Reading Sister Melannie's boo... .... hymn "'Tis the Gift to Be Simple." Her down-to-earth approach gently confirms things we already know while opening our eyes to things we may not know—like the beauty present in ordinary things, such as a swamp or a fire hydrant, and even in brokenness and grief. The book suggests that we, too, have the ability to see the world with the eyes of a poet and to pray with the vision of a prophet. So, prime the pump with a chapter or two from *The Grace of Beauty* and then put on your "Noticing Glasses" and experience our world from a fresh new perspective.

MICHAEL HARTER, SJ, *editor of Hearts on Fire—Praying with Jesuits*

Reading this delightful book is like being led by Sister Melannie into an art gallery where each chapter is a painting of a special manifestation of beauty. She paints each one with an interplay of the colors of her stirring descriptions and examples, quotations from sources throughout the ages, practical applications, and moving questions for our consideration. As each chapter closed with prayer and recommended music, I was filled with joy in the Creator of beauty.

PATRICIA LIVINGSTON, *wife, mother, grandmother; writer, speaker, retreat director*

As I read *The Grace of Beauty* for the first time (it won't be the last), I felt like I was on retreat. Melannie's reflections called me back to the beauty of all life (which I can often take for granted). They urged me to reconnect with myself, others, creation, ordinary things, grief, and God. They challenged me to be a person of compassionate service.

The integration of Scripture; stories; theology; art; music; quotes from saints, philosophers, poets, prophets, and life's ordinary people; prayer; and reflection/conversation questions touches our heads, our hearts, and our hands. *The Grace of Beauty* will enrich your spirit and all your experiences—over and over again.

JANET SCHAEFFLER, OP, *retreat and workshop presenter; author of Let This Be the Time: Spiritual Essentials for Life's Second Act; Deepening Faith: Adult Faith Formation in the Parish; The Spirituality of the Catechist: Feeding Your Soul, Growing in Faith, Sharing with Others*

A gem of a book woven from thoughts, ideas, and concepts of major thinkers, artists, and writers on spirituality. I suggest you read it with pen and pad in hand, for you will surely want to record some of these as you read.

MARY ANN FLANNERY, *Sister of Charity of Cincinnati, retreat director and writer*

MELANNIE SVOBODA, SND

The Grace of Beauty

ITS MYSTERY, POWER, AND DELIGHT IN DAILY LIFE

TWENTY-THIRD PUBLICATIONS

twentythirdpublications.com

DEDICATION

To the newly formed U.S. Province
of the Sisters of Notre Dame

The reflection "The Incarnation" (page 70) was first published in *Give Us This Day*, December 2018. The reflection "I Call You Friend" (page 87) was previously published in *Give Us This Day*, March 2019. The reflection "And the Stalk Said" (page 99) was previously published in *Give Us This Day*, March 2018.

TWENTY-THIRD PUBLICATIONS
One Montauk Avenue, Suite 200
New London, CT 06320
(860) 437-3012 or (800) 321-0411
www.twentythirdpublications.com

Cover photo: ©Shutterstock.com / saras66

ISBN: 978-1-62785-541-9
Printed in the U.S.A.

A division of Bayard, Inc.

Contents

I did not have to ask my heart
what it wanted
because of all desires
I have ever known,
just one did I cling to,
for it was the essence of all desire:
to know beauty.

ST. JOHN OF THE CROSS

INTRODUCTION

You are driving home one evening, and you catch sight of the setting sun, a bright orange disk amid swirls of pink and purple clouds.

Or you are walking in a favorite park when suddenly a doe and her two fawns bound across the path in front of you.

Or you bite into a plump yellow pear and instantly you are transported to a cherished pear tree in your grandparents' back yard.

Or you turn on the car radio and hear the opening strains of a favorite song.

Or you step out onto the back porch in May and catch the faint scent of lilacs.

How do you respond to beauty breaking into your ordinary day? If you are anything like me, you may find yourself whispering a soft "Wow!" or even a heartfelt "Thank you, God!"

Yes, we experience beauty at every turn in life. And the experience of beauty can affect us in many ways. It can stop us in our tracks, lighten our heart, calm our anxiety, ease our pain, move us to tears, or awaken in us the sense that we are part of something much larger than ourselves. Beauty even has the power to draw us to the ultimate source of all beauty, our Creator God or, more accurately, our *Creating* God.

1

Yet we live in a world also beset with ugliness—the ugliness of hatred, division, war, greed, injustices of all kinds, and even violence to this beautiful planet we call home. On a regular basis, then, we must be reminded of our intrinsic need for beauty in our lives. This book is such a reminder. It explores the mystery, power, charm, and illusiveness of beauty. It delves into the relationship of beauty first to God and then to other aspects of our lives, such as love, creation, healing, friendship, morality, service, brokenness, humor, and even grief.

Each chapter in this book consists of an introductory quote, a reflection, and questions for personal or communal sharing. Each chapter concludes with a prayer, poem, or short meditation related to the theme of that chapter. Firmly believing that music can enrich our pondering and prayer, I have also suggested a music video from YouTube for each chapter.

Over sixteen centuries ago, St. Augustine of Hippo, at the time of his conversion, penned those famous words to God, "Late have I loved Thee, O Beauty ever ancient, ever new." His experience of God as Beauty radically altered the trajectory of his life. Our experience of beauty can have a similar impact on us. For the grace of beauty has the power to realign our mind and heart toward the Source of all Beauty, our Beloved God.

prayer

Beautiful God,
be with me as I ponder beauty
in my everyday life.
Help me to grow in my awareness
of the beauty all around me:
in creation, in other people, in myself,
and in human-made beauty expressed in color, line, texture,
word, symbol, sound, gesture, and movement.
Help me to grow in my appreciation of beauty's mystery,
power, delight, and absolute necessity for my life.
Give me the grace to contribute my own
particular beauty to this world—
especially through beauty's highest expression: selfless loving.
I ask these things of you,
"O Beauty ever ancient, ever new." Amen.

CHAPTER I

What Is Beauty?

"I am never more aware of the limitations of language than when I try to describe beauty."

SCOTT RUSSELL SANDERS

B eauty has been defined in many ways. The Greek philosopher Plato saw beauty as the harmony and proportion of parts. His compatriot Aristotle described beauty's chief characteristics as order, symmetry, and definiteness. More recently, the writer Chet Raymo added something to that understanding of beauty. He said that beauty resides in the balance between order and disorder. He was implying, I think, that too much order and symmetry might be more boring than beautiful. So the woman with the updo is made more beautiful by the strand of hair cascading from her otherwise perfectly ordered hairdo.

St. Thomas Aquinas added another dimension to the understanding of beauty when he wrote *pulchra dicuntur quae visa placent.* This means "things that give pleasure when perceived are called beautiful." We perceive beauty through our eyes, yes, but also through our ears, our nose, our touch, our taste. Rachmaninoff's Piano Concerto in B-flat minor is beautiful to hear, while the scent of honeysuckle is beautiful to smell. Many of us find a clean fluffy towel pleasurable to the touch, while a ripe red strawberry is pleasing to the taste. Beauty, then, is that which pleases any of the senses, often more than one at the same time.

Many poets have spoken of beauty's appeal to the senses. In his poem "Each and All," Ralph Waldo Emerson describes several experiences of beauty. One day he was walking near a river when he heard a sparrow singing in a tree. He brought the sparrow home (it takes poetic license to bring a sparrow home!), and the bird continued to sing. But Emerson laments that the experience of beauty fell short of what he had experienced outside. Why? He says, "For I did not bring home the river and the sky—/ He sang to my ear—they sang to my eye." Similarly, while walking on the beach, he gathers a few shells and brings them home, hoping to replicate the beauty of his beach experience. But again, he is disappointed, for the shells "left their beauty on the shore, / With the sun, the sand, and the wild uproar." Emerson concludes: "Nothing is fair or good alone." Things are usually beautiful within a context, that is, in their arrangement with other things.

Beauty can be defined in yet another way. If you look up the word "beauty" on the internet, you will find hundreds of ads for beauty products. Today, beauty has become a $160 billion-a-year global industry! In his book *Love Me*, photographer Zed Nelsen says that "body improvement has become a new religion." Body improvement or body beautification includes things like diets, creams, and makeup of all sorts. It also includes actual surgeries: face-lifts, nose jobs, breast implants, liposuction, and hair restoration, to name a few. There is even a surgery to shorten toes and secure them with metal pins so they fit more easily into three-inch stilettos. (Ouch!) Little wonder Thomas Troeger, professor at Yale Divinity School, laments that beauty has been commercialized and degraded. He writes, "Beauty is reduced to being young, fit, rich, and glamorous." What is needed, he says, is a "theology of beauty."

Any discussion of beauty or a theology of beauty must address this age-old question: Is beauty in the eye of the beholder—as the ancient Greek maxim proposed? My answer to that question is *yes* and *no*. Yes, what we determine is beautiful is somewhat subjective. Our sense of beauty is conditioned by many factors, such as our culture, personal experience, age, gender, education, and religion, to name a few. In some cultures, for example, women are considered beautiful if they are "well-rounded" and have tattooed faces and short-cropped hair. Other cultures deem women beautiful if they have very thin bodies, clear complexions, and long silky hair (preferably blonde). What constitutes beauty in music will vary from person to person too. The music that brings pleasure to a fifty-five-year-old might be quite different from the music that delights a teenager. What constitutes "a beautiful day in the neighborhood" might be conditioned by where the neighborhood is: Miami, Peoria, Honolulu, or Nome. So yes, to an extent, beauty is in the eye of the beholder.

At the same time there are some things that many people, if not most people, would label beautiful. What about the sight of the *aurora borealis*, or polar lights, in the night sky? Or a painting like Girl with a Pearl Earring by Johannes Vermeer? Or the gentle plucking of a harp? Or Harper Lee's powerful novel *To Kill a Mockingbird*? Or the smell and taste of freshly baked bread? The fact is some things seem almost objectively beautiful.

Earlier in this chapter, we noted Aquinas's definition of beauty. Beauty gives us pleasure, he said. In other words, beauty has an effect on us. In the next chapter we will explore some of the specific ways beauty affects us.

Questions for Reflection

1. How do you define or describe beauty?   *leaves*

2. Have you ever had an experience where beauty was definitely in the eye of the beholder? Can you name some things that are considered beautiful by most people?   *a newborn baby*

3. Recall an experience of beauty you have had recently. What made it beautiful? What effect did this experience of beauty have on you?

Thank You, God, for Beauty

Thank you, God, for beauty.
for harmony and proportion,
for order, symmetry, and definiteness,
and for the balance of order and disorder.
Thank you for the pleasure beauty gives us,
the pleasure to our eyes, ears, nose, touch, and taste.
Thank you for oceans and snowflakes,
for giraffes and ladybugs,
for watercolor paintings and clay pots,
for movies, plays, and photographs,
for chirping birds and grand symphonies,
for the scent of roses and the smell of rain,
for the feel of clean sheets and a toddler's hug,
for the taste of a hot cup of coffee or a cold bottle of beer.
Thank you, God, for beauty in all its forms
and the pleasure it bestows on us.
For we believe that all the beauty we experience
is but a faint reflection of you, O Most Beautiful One. Amen.

Digital Connection

Suggested YouTube video: "Creation Calls" by Brian Doerkson

CHAPTER 2

How Beauty Affects Us

"To call something beautiful is not just to describe it, but to react to it."

GORDON GRAHAM

Two old friends were walking down the road one evening when they began to argue. As they went along, they shouted at one another as each tried to impose his view on the other. The longer they argued, the angrier they became. Suddenly, one of them caught sight of the setting sun. He pointed it out to his friend. Immediately the men ceased their arguing. They stood side by side in silence, gazing at the wonder and beauty of the sunset. Several minutes later, when the sun had slipped beneath the horizon, the two friends started on their way again. Only now, having forgotten what they had been arguing about, they walked together cheerfully and at peace with one another.

Beauty affects us. It causes a reaction in us. In this case, the beauty of the sunset made the men stop walking. It silenced them. It engaged them. And, in the end, it brought peace between them.

In this chapter, we will explore some of the affects beauty can have on us. We will start with beauty's effect on the human brain.

Researchers at the University College London, a public research institution, have actually measured the effect of beauty on the brain. In one study, they hooked up electrodes to peoples' heads to measure blood flow in various parts of the brain. Then they showed these people a series of pictures and asked them to rate each picture as beautiful or not. When people rated the picture as beautiful, something interesting happened. One part of their brain "lit up"; that is, there was an increase in blood flow to that part of the brain, the *medial orbitofrontal cortex*. This part of the brain serves several functions. Mainly it is involved with emotions and the ability to make decisions. Further research is needed to understand the significance of this data. Nevertheless, the research does show that the experience of beauty has an actual physical impact on the brain.

It is no surprise, then, that beauty can affect our psychological and spiritual well-being. Thomas Moore, in is classic book *Care of the Soul*, argues that beauty is absolutely essential for the health of the soul. In fact, he goes so far as to say that if our lives lack beauty, we will probably suffer from familiar disturbances, such as depression or a sense of meaninglessness. The soul craves beauty, says Moore, and in its absence, it suffers what James Hillman has called "beauty neurosis." If this is true, then we should be mindful of injecting regular "doses of beauty" into our lives. We should also be concerned about the long-term effect on individuals deprived of beauty through poverty, violence, war, natural disasters, incarceration, or living for years in refugee camps.

Let us now look more closely at some of the other effects beauty can have on us. First, beauty can slow us down. How often has a beautiful sunset slowed people down—or actually made then stop and gaze at it? It is as if beauty has the power to ensnare us, to distract us from doing what we were doing. Here is an example of beauty ensnaring me. I pull into the parking lot at the grocery store when one of my favorite songs or pieces of music is playing on my car radio. If it is the "oldie station," it might be Andy Williams's "Moon River" or Frank Sinatra's "New York." If it is the classical station, it could be Mozart's "A Little Night Music" or Beethoven's "Moonlight Sonata." What do I do? Do I switch off the car engine and go into the store? No. I switch off the car, yes, but only partway so my radio stays on. Then I sit in my car and listen to the musical selection until it is finished. For me, the beauty of the music has "hooked me" and made me pause in the middle of my work.

Beauty's power to lure people away from their ordinary tasks is demonstrated every time there is a solar eclipse. When this phenomenon occurs, millions of people leave work, gather in public places, and don special glasses to take in the mystery and beauty of such an event. A harvest moon will likewise lure people out of their cozy homes to get a better look at the giant orange orb rising on the horizon. The sighting of an eagle or blue heron also tempts people to stop and stare. A good question to ask ourselves is this: What kind of beauty do we pause for?

Studies have also shown that beauty can lift our spirits and ease our stress. A visit to an art museum, attendance at a concert, a stroll along the beach, the taste of a favorite meal, the smell of gardenias, or the sight of a mother duck swimming with her brood of ducklings—all have a way of lifting our hearts or calming our spirits.

Beauty can also unite us with other people. We feel at one with others, whether we are watching fireworks on the Fourth of July, cheering for our favorite sports team, enjoying the music of a local band on the town square, or singing Christmas carols at midnight Mass. Yes, beauty has the power to unite us as few other things can.

11

And finally, beauty can be a pathway to God. I experienced this a few years ago when I learned that a dear friend of mine, a Sister of Notre Dame, had fallen and broken her hip. She was far from home, attending an educational conference when this happened, complicating her ordeal. I was beside myself with worry for her. A few other sisters and two laywomen were now looking after her in the hospital, and they promised to keep me updated. Meanwhile, I made plans to make the five-hour drive with another sister to be with her after her surgery.

That night I was restless as I kept worrying about her. The next morning, as soon as I got up, I went into my office next door where I keep a coffee maker. I turned it on. As I did, I glanced out the third-floor window into our back yard. In the semi-darkness, I detected movement. Then I saw four deer leisurely nibbling on the grass below. A soft "Oh!" escaped my lips as I gazed down upon them. I had never seen them in our yard before! As I watched them, I felt a Presence much larger than myself. I sensed that this Presence, this Power, this Force was holding everything in existence—including these beautiful deer—and my beautiful friend. This God was sustaining her, watching over her, and caring for her. I need not fear. The sight of those deer—untamed and free—gave me peace and strength by uniting me to the Source of their beauty, our loving Creator God.

Beauty affects us. It slows us down. It eases our anxiety. It unites us with each other. It is a pathway to God. Psychologists say that beauty also has the power to heal us. We will explore that topic in the next chapter.

Questions for Reflection

double rainbow in Hawaii

1. Have you experienced beauty's power to slow you down or even stop you? If so, when and how?

2. Have you experienced beauty's power to lift your spirits, ease your stress, or be a pathway to God? If so, when and how?

3. If beauty is so important for physical and spiritual well-being, how can you inject regular doses of beauty into your everyday life?

Prayer for Beauty

Come, Beauty, slow me down.
Stop me in my tracks.
Come, Beauty, and lure me away from my work,
my stress, my constant worrying.
Lift my spirits; ease my anxieties.
Help me to experience the vastness of the created world
of which I am a tiny but significant part.
Make me more attentive to the beauty that surrounds me,
the beauty of the extraordinary and the beauty of the everyday.
Come, Beauty, be a pathway for me to God,
Our Creator, Our Sustainer, Our Beloved One. Amen.

Digital Connection

Suggested YouTube: "For the Beauty of the Earth" (John Rutter with lyrics), performed by the St. Phillip's Boys Choir

CHAPTER 3

The Healing Power of Beauty

*"Beauty gives [us] the feeling of homecoming,
aliveness, wholesomeness, and connection.
Beauty possesses the power to heal souls."*

JEAN MAALOUF

D oes beauty really possess the power to heal?

To answer that question, let us begin with "Sister Joan's" story. When Joan was about forty, her doctor discovered a mass on her kidney. It was either a harmless cyst or a cancerous tumor. The doctor ordered several tests and prepared Joan for the worst. While waiting for the test results, Joan became very anxious and fearful. A few days later, she received the doctor's report: the mass was a cyst.

Joan was greatly relieved, but she was shaken by the ordeal. Two weeks later, when she made a retreat, she was still teary-eyed and heavy-hearted. After talking with her director, she decided that, during the retreat, she would visit "a pretty place" every afternoon. She said, "I had the feeling that beauty would heal me." One afternoon she drove to the city's botanical gardens, ten acres of beautiful flowers in full bloom. As she slowly walked the pathways, she was immersed in beauty with every step. As she strolled along, she felt something happening within her. "I experienced a deep peace pouring into me," she said. "Gradually I found myself being healed of my fear and anxiety." Later she described the experience as "an anointing."

Spiritual director Linda Parnell writes, "The regular, intentional inclusion of beauty into one's life has the power to heal our lives and transform our way of 'seeing' the world." She speaks not only from her ministry of directing others but also from her own experience. At one point in her life, she found herself with an "unexplained persistent cough." Greatly overworked and lacking in sleep, she realized she was on the verge of serious burnout. Through her personal prayer and the encouragement of her adult daughter, Parnell resigned her position and began the slow work of recuperation. She started by intentionally introducing elements of beauty back into her daily life. She created a visual journal of things around her that she was naturally drawn to. She says, "I began to notice a new way of seeing beauty." Along with this new way of seeing came "an increased sense of creativity. The effects of both have proven transformative." She was eventually able to return to work, but she was a changed and wiser woman—thanks to beauty.

Many Christian churches, especially the Catholic and Orthodox Churches, have a history of emphasizing the importance of beauty. Currently I help with the RCIA at St. Mary Parish in Chardon, Ohio. I have given the presentation on Mary for several years. During the talk, I show various artistic representations of the annunciation—from the traditional (Mary kneeling on a prie-dieu) to the contemporary (Mary wearing saddle shoes). I always conclude my talk with a "field trip" into the church. Once there, we look for all the artistic representations of Mary we can find. In doing so, we all (myself included) come to a greater appreciation of the simple beauty of our church—the wooden pews, stained-glass windows, dark wood altar, statues, icons, stations of the cross, wall hanging, sanctuary lamp. It is easy to see why some people come to Mass early not only to pray but also just to *be* with all that beauty.

We might be wondering, how does the healing power of beauty work. There are, no doubt, a number of ways. We will look at three of them.

First, *beauty grounds us*. It asks us for our full attention. When we are entranced by beauty, we are rooted in the here and now. A lovely sunset, for example, requests our attention in the present moment. We cannot make it happen any sooner than the appointed time. We cannot put off watching it for even fifteen minutes, for it will be gone by then. To enjoy a sunset we cannot be doing other things—like figuring out a solution to a problem, or carrying on a deep conversation with another, or texting. When beauty grounds us, it simultaneously *affirms life*. In his book *Beauty and the Soul*, Piero Ferrucci writes, "The more we can perceive beauty in our surroundings and also inside us, the more we feel at home and glad to exist."

Second, *beauty stimulates the imagination*. When we feel overwhelmed by our problems or imprisoned by our circumstances, beauty has a way of activating our imagination. Beauty can lead us to see things in a different way and to envision new possibilities. Recently I saw a short documentary on YouTube titled *Landfill Harmonic*. It tells the story of a group of young people living next to a garbage dump in Cateura, Paraguay. Most of their families eke out a living by picking things out of the garbage and selling them. Amazingly, these children have made musical instruments from objects they found in the trash. A cello, for example, was made from a large oilcan and pieces of discarded wood. Most of the children live in extreme poverty, but they play beautiful classical music on their recycled instruments. One girl said, "My life would be meaningless without music." It was the beauty of music that led them to find an imaginative way to form an orchestra and to produce music of their own.

Third, *beauty eases our sense of aloneness.* As I mentioned earlier, beauty connects us to others—and to *the* Other, namely, God. When we experience the beautiful, we feel our oneness with each other. This experience of connectedness to others can ease the sense of isolation often associated with depression, pain, and sorrow. And the experience of oneness with God convinces us that whatever we are experiencing in our life—whether ugly, beautiful, or something in between—we are being held in God's loving embrace.

Questions for Reflection

1. Have you ever had an experience of beauty's healing power? If so, reflect on this experience. What were the circumstances? What beauty did you experience? How did you feel after your experience with beauty?

2. Do you regularly and intentionally include beauty in your life? If so, how do you do this? If not, what is hindering you from doing this?

3. How aware are you of the beauty of your place of worship. Next time you go to church, look around and notice things you would label beautiful. Are there any aspects of the worship environment that you believe distract from the beauty?

Poppies Make Good Doctors

I have it on good authority:
Poppies make good doctors.
Dr. Rollo May, renowned psychologist,
tells this story. As a young man,
he suffered a nervous breakdown.
In his gloom and distress, he went for a walk one day
and came upon a field of red poppies.
Almost as far as the eye could see,
they stood there in their humble splendor,
gently bobbing in the sun.
Dr. May walked into their midst,
until he was knee-deep in poppies.
For several minutes he stood with them,
basking in their good company.
Later he wrote, "I just stood there,
intoxicated, wholly captivated by the poppies."

Prior to this experience,
he had been too busy to "waste his time"
looking at flowers.
But now, in his utter desolation,
he needed their beauty
to bring himself back to life.

Later he said of his poppy experience:
"Beauty kept me alive."

Digital Connection

Suggested YouTube video: "Abide with Me" by Carrie Newcomer and Parker J. Palmer

CHAPTER 4

Beauty's Relationship to God

"God is beauty itself."

ST. THOMAS AQUINAS

W hat is the relationship of beauty to God? Over the centuries, theologians and other writers have given us different ways to express this relationship. Some have said things like, "God is the source of all beauty." If God is the source of all that is, then certainly God is the source of beauty. The astronomer Carl Sagan said, "If you want to make an apple pie from scratch, you first have to create the universe." If you want to make something beautiful—a poem, a painting, a piano concerto—you will rely on components that are already in existence: a human brain that has the capacity for language and creativity; eyes that can perceive color, texture, depth; and ears that can detect and appreciate sound. So, yes, we can say that God is the source of all beauty.

But there are many other ways of describing God's relationship to beauty. We will briefly look at a few of them. First, *beauty is another name for God.* Our Judeo-Christian tradition bestows many names on God. We will look at some of those specific names in a later chapter. But here we begin with the beautiful words of St. Augustine. He addressed God as "O Beauty ever ancient, ever new." Some contemporary theologians feel we Christians need to reclaim God as Beauty. For too long, they say, our faith has placed too much emphasis on God as Truth and Goodness. This emphasis has made our faith at times too preoccupied with correct doctrine (truth) and proper behavior (goodness.) But by addressing God as Beauty, our relationship with God might be characterized more by awe, pleasure, joy, delight, and gratitude.

Father John Navone, SJ, has written a beautiful book on beauty. I personally love the title: *Enjoying God's Beauty*. He emphasizes that our relationship with God should be characterized by delight and enjoyment. (When was the last time you heard a homily on *enjoying* God?) We must enjoy Jesus too—especially his beauty. Navone says this about Jesus: "We cannot know Jesus in the biblical sense without knowing the beauty of his true goodness." Later in this book, we will reflect on the beauty of Jesus.

There are other ways to express beauty's relationship to God. The writer Macrina Wiederkehr, OSB, says, *"Beauty is one of God's faces."* Hardly anything more readily identifies a person than their face (think of facial recognition technology). If beauty is God's face, then beauty, to an extent, identifies who God is. But notice: Wiederkehr says beauty is *one* of God's faces.

Ralph Waldo Emerson described God's relation to beauty in this way: *"Beauty is God's handwriting."* Our handwriting is unique to us. Handwriting experts can even tell if a signature is authentic or not. Some people go so far as to claim that our handwriting can reveal significant clues about our personality—whether we are friendly, cautious, disciplined, playful, and so forth. At this time, it is still too early to see to what extent that may be true. But it is fun to ask: What does the beauty of creation reveal about God's "personality"? For me, it reveals (among other things) that our Creator is highly imaginative, sensitive, powerful, playful, and a lover of diversity.

In his book, *Gardening Eden*, Michael Abbate says, "*Beauty is the shadow of God.*" This statement captures some of the mystery and even illusiveness of God. Do you remember how, as a child, you were fascinated by your shadow? Perhaps you danced with it, you made it do funny things, or you even tried to run away from it. Your shadow belonged to you in a way, but it was not you. You were much more than the shadow you cast on a sunny day.

Two other images of beauty's relationship to God are similar. Cardinal Godfried Danneels of Brussels says, "*Beauty is a door that leads to God.*" Philosopher Ernst Cassirer writes, "*Beauty is a bridge to God.*" Both images view beauty as a means to approach God. Beauty is something we can enter or cross over to reach Divinity.

Another image of God's relationship to beauty is *God as the potter*. It is a venerable scriptural image. God is the potter who fashioned our beautiful world—including us. But once the potter is finished making the pot, the pot is separated from the potter—except that the pot bears the mark of the potter's hand. In her book *Radical Optimism*, Beatrice Bruteau prefers not to think of God as a potter, but *God as a dancer*. In her view, "The whole world is the Creator's expressive gesture. God is in the world as the dancer is in the dance. The dance *is* the dancer, dancing." This image does not separate creation from the Creator. It also underscores the fact that creation is not a past event. Rather, it is an ever-continuing act of God.

I tried to come up with my own image that depicts beauty's relationship to God. I first thought, "Beauty is the breath of God." A breath is synonymous with life itself. A breath is also invisible. But as I reflected on this image, I modified it: *Beauty is God breathing*. To me this image says: God is very much alive. Even if you cannot see God, God is breathing in all the beauty God has created.

For me, beauty says, "We are not alone. God is here, with and among us. Come, let us enjoy God!"

Questions for Reflection

1. Of all the images given in this chapter, are there any you are drawn to? Why or why not?

2. To what extent is your relationship with God characterized by "awe, pleasure, joy, delight, and gratitude"?

3. Is there any other image of the relationship between beauty and God that you like? It can be one you have read or heard, or one you came up with yourself.

Let Me Call You Beauty

Let me call you Beauty, O Divine One.
Let me be in awe of you.
Let me take delight in you.
Let me enjoy you,
while growing in gratitude for who you are
and for all you do.
When I chance upon beauty in my ordinary days,
let me see it as one of your faces.
Help me to cherish beauty in all its forms
as I cherish the handwriting of a loved one.
Whenever I encounter beauty,
remind me that beauty is but a shadow of you,
passing by me, over me, beneath me, through me.
Help me to see beauty as a door that opens to you,
as a bridge I can cross over to be wholly in your presence.
May I see all the beauty that surrounds me
as you, dancing your dance of wonder and delight.
May I make time to notice and enjoy
the beauty in my everyday life and, in the process,
feel you breathing new life into me
and into the whole world. Amen.

Digital Connection

Suggested YouTube video: "You Alone"
by Daniel and Catherine Lovett

CHAPTER 5

The Holy Here and Now

*"Beauty and grace are performed
whether or not we will sense them.
The least we can do is try to be there."*

ANNIE DILLARD

I recently read an article in which the author lamented the "disappearance of here." With our smart phones and other electronic devices, he said, we can easily be somewhere else rather than where we actually are.

The article was accompanied by a photo of three young college women sitting on the lawn on campus beneath some lovely trees. The scene looks idyllic until you notice that the women are not conversing with each other or even enjoying the beauty surrounding them. Instead, with their heads bent down, they are all texting on their cellphones. In a way, we can say: they are no longer *here*; that is, they are no longer with each other under the beautiful canopy of trees.

The disappearance of *here* is often accompanied by the disappearance of *now*. These two losses can have serious consequences. How many car accidents have been attributed to drivers using their phones? And what about that woman texting while walking in the mall who stumbled right into a fountain of water? She said she never saw it. Understandably, because she was no longer present to her here and now.

I am not against cellphones or other electronic devices, of course. I too enjoy the convenience, companionship, and security they provide. But I believe there is a time for turning them off— while driving, during meals, at a movie, in church, while strolling in a park, while relaxing with family and friends.

In the early eighteenth century, the French Jesuit Jean Pierre de Caussade coined the phrase "the sacrament of the present moment." Notice he called the here and now a *sacrament*. Why? Because it is in the here and now that we primarily encounter God and God's will for us. Caussade wrote: "The divine will is a deep abyss of which the present moment is the entrance." Another French writer, a twentieth-century laywoman, Simone Weil, said something similar. She warned against "daydreaming." By daydreaming she meant "not being present to where one is." Weil says that love requires we embrace life as it is, by showing up in the here and now.

If we are inattentive to the here and now, we miss a lot of beauty too. What can cause us to be unmindful of the present moment besides our cellphones? Rushing can. "Hurry sickness" is now a recognized phenomenon in medical circles. It is the constant feeling of urgency that causes rushing or trying to do too many things at once. "Hurry sickness" can cause high blood pressure, ulcers, and tension headaches. It often saps the joy out of life. We might add, rushing and multitasking all the time can sap the beauty out of life too. One antidote for "hurry sickness" is simply to slow down.

In his book *In Praise of Slowness*, Carl Honore calls himself a "recovering speedaholic." One day he found himself annoyed while reading a bedtime story to his four-year-old boy. Honore preferred a brief story read quickly. After all, he was a busy man. But his son preferred "long stories read at a slow meandering pace." Then one day Honore saw an ad for books of "one-minute bedtime stories." He was ready to place an order, when he suddenly stopped, realizing what he was doing with his life. He writes, "My whole life has turned into an exercise in hurry, in packing more and more into every hour. I am Scrooge with a stopwatch, obsessed with saving every last scrap of time, a minute here, a few seconds there. And I am not alone." In time, Honore became a leading spokesperson for the so-called "Slow Movement."

Advocates of the "Slow Movement" are not against speed per se. If speed is appropriate for a certain activity, then that's fine. But, they say, speed has become an addiction, almost a kind of idolatry. Some things deserve to be done slowly—like reading a bedtime story, eating a meal, walking the dog, stirring the tapioca, conversing with a friend.

Another factor that can distract us from the present moment is busyness. Busyness means more than merely working. Busyness connotes having too many things to do, which results in franticness—as when you yell at someone, "Don't bother me now! Can't you see I'm busy?" Busyness can inhibit our awareness of beauty by restricting us to the surface of life. When we are busy, we can be so focused on the task at hand that we lose sight of our surroundings—the beautiful smile of the checkout clerk, the soft babbling of a toddler in the back of church, the gently falling snow outside our window. By pausing regularly in whatever we are doing, we can reconnect to the here and now.

By pausing amid our busyness, we can also connect with the deeper meaning of what we do. St. Ignatius of Loyola encouraged this practice. Throughout his day, he regularly paused and asked himself, "What are you doing?" He might answer, "I am walking down this hallway." But why? "Because I'm going to the dining room." Why? "Because I need physical nourishment." Why? "So I may have strength to do God's work." By reflecting on the deeper significance of what we are doing, we might eventually answer something like this: "I am doing these tasks out of love for my family... to support my family... to help other people... for the good of the environment... for the love of God."

And finally, in this discussion of the "holy here and now," we must remember this: Periodic "escapes" from our here and now are not only necessary but also healthy. It is good to get lost in a book or movie, listen to your favorite music, take a mini-vacation, or even make a religious retreat. When we make a retreat, for example, we are "escaping" our ordinary here and now and replacing it with the here and now of prayer, silence, solitude, and reflection. But the purpose of all our "escapes" is to enable us to return to our ordinary here and now with greater energy, enthusiasm, courage, vision, and (above all) love.

Questions for Reflection

1. On a scale of 1 to 10, (1 = not aware and 10 = very aware) answer this: Ordinarily how aware are you of the here and now?

2. Do you tend to be a "speedaholic"? If so, how might you take pauses in your work to connect with the beauty and/or deeper meaning of what you are doing?

3. Have you ever experienced the present moment as a sacrament, as holy? If so, reflect on or share this experience. When did it happen? How did it make you feel?

Prayer for the Present Moment

Loving God, author of all time and place,
I ask for a greater awareness of the here and now
and a deeper appreciation for the present moment.
Help me to see the here and now as a sacrament, as holy,
and as the entrance to your divine will for me.
May I not succumb to the "hurry sickness"
by always rushing around and trying to do
too many things at once.
May I not worship the false gods of speed and busyness.
Help me to take pauses throughout my day
to reconnect with the world and the people around me
and to remember the deeper meaning of all I do:
love for family, for other people, and for you.
I ask for these graces in the name of Jesus
who paused to notice the birds soaring in the air
and the wildflowers bobbing in the fields. Amen.

Digital Connection

Suggested YouTube: "Everyday God" by Bernadette Farrell

CHAPTER 6

Useless Beauty

*"The universe...is a single
gorgeous celebratory event."*

THOMAS BERRY

Scott Russell Sanders, professor emeritus of English at Indiana University, has written an article for the *Notre Dame Magazine* (August 2012) titled "Useless Beauty." In it, he differentiates between beauty that seems to have a definite purpose and beauty that does not seem to serve a specific function.

Sanders observed this distinction after studying beauty in the natural world. He concluded that some beauty seems specifically designed to increase the chances of survival for specific organisms as well as whole species. The peacock's tail, for example, is attractive to mates. This encourages amorous behavior among the peafowl, which results in lots of baby peacocks (called peachicks). The zebra's stripes confuse predators and enable zebras to escape death more readily. The monarch butterfly's bright orange and black wings shout to predators, "I'm poison! Don't eat me!" thus enabling them to live for another day. The beauty of blinking lightning bugs, the courtship dance of sandhill cranes, and the chirping of the frogs in spring can all be viewed as useful beauty, as purposeful.

But what about useless beauty, that is, beauty that seems to have no purpose—except to be? Sanders lists a host of examples of useless beauty such as the pearly interior of the nautilus shell. No one sees this beauty—except the nautilus. But now, he says, there is a two-legged predator who collects these shells, and slices them in half, thus exposing their lovely interior for other two-legged predators to see and buy! Thus, this useless beauty is now useful—for some humans to make money and for others to beautify their homes.

The interior of geodes is another example of useless beauty. On the outside, geodes are brownish-grayish lumps of sediment. But crack them open and you will find beautiful colors of orange, purple, blue, and red. Then there are all those flowers. Yes, we know that the color, scent, and shape of many flowers are designed to attract pollinators who are essential for the flower's reproduction. But are not some flowers much fancier than they need to be—fuchsia, bleeding hearts, wild columbine, the iris, to name a few?

And what about all the other useless beauty found in the non-living world? What about sunrises and sunsets, the northern lights, the stars, the vast expanse of sea with its steady pounding against the shore? What about clouds, rainbows, waterfalls, glaciers, mountains, canyons? Look around and you will see useless beauty everywhere!

We might ask: What does all this beauty—whether useful or useless—reveal about the Creator? Says Sanders, "The Designer must be inordinately fond of beauty." I like that! God is *inordinately fond* of beauty. If we believe this, then we must conclude that beauty is good. Very, very good. More than that, beauty is holy and deserving of our care. Unfortunately, we humans do not always view beauty with tenderness and respect. We can trace a more utilitarian attitude toward nature all the way back to Genesis.

Genesis gives two different accounts of creation. The first account, found in the first chapter of Genesis, begins with God at work creating the cosmos. The work of creation is divided into periods of time called days. At the end of each day, what does the Creator do? The Creator rests. The Creator also pronounces everything made on each day as *good*. More than one Scripture scholar has suggested that the Hebrew word for *good* used in this instance could also be translated *beautiful*. Genesis could read, "Then God said, 'Let there be light,' and there was light. God saw how *beautiful* the light was" (Gn 1:3–4).

God then creates Adam and Eve on the sixth day, saying to them, "Have dominion over the fish of the sea, the birds of the air, and all living things that move on the earth" (Gn 1:28). The use of the word *dominion* here is an unfortunate word choice. For too many centuries, we Christians have used that word *dominion* to assert humankind's superiority over all creation. We have thought that the natural world is ours to control and dispose of as we see fit. As a result, we have committed all kinds of atrocities to planet earth, from polluting our air, to exterminating whole species of animals, destroying our rain forests, and using our rivers and oceans as garbage dumps. Some Scripture translations do not use the word *dominion*. But they use similar words like *rule over*, *reign over*, or *take charge of*.

But if we read the second account of creation, found in Genesis 2, we find different words used. God puts Adam in the Garden of Eden "to cultivate and care for it" (Gn 2:15). Other translations say this: *dress it and keep it, serve it and keep it, cultivate it and guard it, tend it and watch over it.* Cultivating, caring, tending, and watching over the earthly garden connotes far more respect than dominating or ruling over it. Caring presupposes an appreciation and reverence for the beautiful earthly world of which we are a part.

Unfortunately, a certain utilitarian ethic is present in our world today, perhaps more than ever. This ethic says that nothing has value unless it is *useful*—especially to humans. This ethic seeps into personal relationships, congressional legislation, international policies, and even our buying habits. Fortunately, there is another ethic in our world that believes and upholds concepts like these: We did not make nature; nature made us. We are not masters of the earth; we are *members* of the earth community. Some things are of inestimable value simply because they are.

Poet Ralph Waldo Emerson wrote a poem that expresses the value of beauty for its own sake. The poem is called "The Rhodora" (a rhodora is a pinkish purple plant found in northeastern North America). One day, while walking through the woods in May, Emerson comes upon a rhodora. He muses, "Why is the flower's beauty wasted on the earth and sky?" He decides, "beauty is its own excuse for being." He also feels and expresses his divine connectedness to the flower in these words: "The self-same power that brought me there, brought you."

Questions for Reflection

1. Can you give some examples of useful beauty?

2. What evidence supports the theory that God "must be inordinately fond of beauty"?

3. Do your daily choices, habits, and practices reflect a utilitarian ethic toward creation or a more caring one? Or both?

In Praise of Useless Beauty

Creator God, this we believe:
beautiful things need not be useful to have great worth.
Sunrises, sunsets, rainbows,
the northern lights, the Grand Canyon,
have worth simply because of their beauty.
A violet growing shyly in a forest glen
is valuable even though only one lone hiker
will ever see it there.
This also we believe:
We are meant to tend, watch over, serve, guard, and care for
our beautiful earthly home.
We are not to be rulers over creation;
we are to be good stewards.
We are not to be masters of this world;
we are to be members of one earthly community.
Creator God, we thank you for being
inordinately fond of beauty.
May we be made more and more into your image. Amen.

Digital Connection

Suggested YouTube video: "God of Wonders"
by Third Day Worship Video with lyrics

CHAPTER 7

The Beauty and Power of Metaphor

*"The best metaphors always [give] both
a shock and a shock of recognition."*

SALLIE MCFAGUE

We use metaphors all the time. We say things like this: "I'm as hungry as a bear... She's an angel... I have too much on my plate right now." Simply put, a metaphor is a figure of speech that identifies similarities between two different entities. When we say, "She's an angel," for example, we are not saying she is a *real* angel. No, she is a human being, but she has some of the qualities we imagine an angel might have, such as goodness, love, and tenderness.

Poets use metaphors all the time. Emily Dickinson wrote "Hope is a thing with feathers," comparing hope to a bird that "perches in the soul" and sings without end. In Sonnet 18, William Shakespeare asks his beloved, "Shall I compare thee to a summer day?" He then proceeds to do just that, comparing his beloved to the beauty and fairness of a day in summer. Carl Sandburg wrote,

"The fog comes/ on little cat feet," likening the way the fog comes into the harbor to the movement of a cat—silent, slow, mysterious.

The French philosopher Paul Ricoeur says the beauty of metaphors lies in their "surplus of meaning." In other words, metaphors are not merely synonyms. They offer additional knowledge, suggestions, and nuances that go beyond their literal meaning. When the psalmist says, "The Lord is my shepherd," he is attributing to God some of the qualities of a good shepherd, such as vigilance, care, and protection. The power of metaphor lies in its ability to influence or shape our thought. To call God shepherd can affect our way of thinking about God and relating to God.

Jesus was a master of metaphor. He used metaphors to describe himself: "I am the bread of life... the light of the world... the good shepherd... friend." One of his most famous metaphorical descriptions of himself is "I am the vine, you are the branches" (Jn 15:5). What does this metaphor imply about the relationship between Jesus and us, his disciples? It implies that the relationship is an organic relationship, a living thing that grows and develops. We, the branches, derive our vitality and strength from Jesus, the vine. If we do not remain connected to Jesus, we can wither and die.

Jesus used metaphors when describing the kingdom of God. He said the kingdom was like a mustard seed, yeast, a net, a treasury. One of his most surprising metaphors for the kingdom was a wedding feast. This metaphor suggests the kingdom is a gathering of happy people celebrating a joyful occasion. There's camaraderie, good food and drink, music and dancing, fun and relaxation. The power of Jesus' metaphors lies in his use of ordinary and familiar things, things people could relate to—even centuries later.

Scripture is replete with metaphors for God. But since God is so far beyond anything we could ever say about God, all our metaphors are limited. At the same time, however, each metaphor can give us some insights into who God is. One problem is that we often focus on only a few of the biblical images of God, such as King, Lord, Rock, Father, Shepherd, thus depriving ourselves of a richer relationship with the Divine.

Lauren Winner, an Episcopal priest, has written *Wearing God*, a book about metaphors for God. Winner's book explores scriptural images or metaphors for God often overlooked by many believers. What metaphors? God as clothing, smell, bread, laughter, flame, and a woman in labor. Are you familiar with any of these metaphors? Maybe not. It is the image of God as a woman in labor that I would like to say a few words about here.

A clear description of this image of God is found in Isaiah 42:14 where God says through the prophet: "For a long time I have held my peace, I have kept still and restrained myself; now I cry out like a woman in labor, I will gasp and pant." These words were written when a significant part of the Judean population was living in exile in Babylon with little hope of returning home. In the wake of such a catastrophe, Isaiah's words were meant to assure the people that God was with them even now—in their pain, a pain that would eventually lead to birth and new life. Through this beautiful metaphor, God through Isaiah was offering the people hope in the midst of their anguish.

Other Scripture passages echo this image of God as a laboring woman. The psalmist puts these words into God's mouth: "From the womb before the day star I begot thee" (Ps 110:3, *Douay-Rheims* translation). Later Isaiah gives the people these tender words from God: "Can a mother forget her infant [nursing child], be without tenderness for the child of her womb? Even should she forget, I will never forget you" (Is 49:15). Here God is portrayed not only as a woman who gives birth, but also as a mother who nurses her child.

Some people might be uneasy or even disturbed by the image of

God as a laboring woman, groaning and writhing in pain. Are we uncomfortable with a God so utterly vulnerable and so seemingly out of control? But Winner maintains that such an image suggests that "God chooses to participate in the work of new creation with bellowing and panting." This reminds us that God somehow is with us in our pain. And God, through Jesus, continues to nourish us with his own body, the Eucharist, as a mother nourishes her child.

The image of God as a laboring woman and a nursing mother implies that God is working hard to bring forth redemption. Another implication of this metaphor: if I am participating with God in this great work, then I too will experience times of gasping and moaning and panting. I too will know periods of pain and vulnerability and loss of control—just as Jesus did.

Winner concludes her chapter on God as laboring woman with a prayer by St. Anselm of Canterbury. Written in the eleventh century, this prayer, addressed to Jesus, employs a feminine metaphor for Jesus that Jesus himself gave us (Mt 23:37):

> And you, Jesus, are you not also a mother?
> Are you not the mother who, like a hen,
> Gathers her chicks under her wings?...
> It is by your death that [we] have been born.

All metaphors and images of God, though incomplete, can offer us glimpses of who God is. In so doing, they can enrich our relationship with the One whose love for us is not only beyond words but beyond measure.

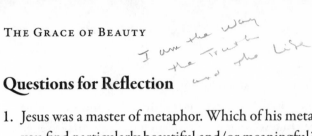

Questions for Reflection

1. Jesus was a master of metaphor. Which of his metaphors do you find particularly beautiful and/or meaningful? Why?

2. What metaphors for God do you find especially meaningful? Why?

3. What do you think or feel about the metaphor of God as a woman in labor or as a nursing mother? Why?

Jesus, Master of Metaphor

Jesus, Master of Metaphor,
you saw the interconnectedness of all things.
You compared yourself to Living Water,
a mother hen, the Way, the Truth, the Life.
You compared us to beloved children,
sheep without a shepherd, friends.
You said we were more precious than many sparrows,
more beautiful than all the wildflowers dancing in the field.

You said the way was sometimes a narrow gate,
a rocky path, a road where robbers lurked.
But you also said, "Fear not" for "I am the Way."

Jesus, Master of Metaphor,
help me to share your vision more and more,
a vision that detects God's amazing love
even in the ordinary workings of the natural world
and in the familiar things of everyday life.

Help me to share in your work of redemption,
trusting that the anguish I may experience at times
will lead to new birth and new life. Amen.

Digital Connection

Suggested YouTube video: "I Will Never Forget You, My People" sung by Richard Carney

CHAPTER 8

Names of God

"Many are the names of God, and infinite the forms through which God may be approached."

RAMAKRISHNA, NINETEENTH-CENTURY HINDU MYSTIC

I n the preceding chapter we explored the beauty and power of metaphor. We looked at Jesus' use of metaphor in his teachings. Then we explored a few biblical metaphors for God, homing in on God as laboring woman. In this chapter we will focus on some of the names of God.

In the tradition of Islam, there are at least ninety-nine names of Allah. The names are also called the attributes of Allah. Some of these names are found only in the *Quran (Koran)*. Others are found only in the *hadith*. The *hadith* is a collection of traditions containing the sayings of the Prophet Mohammad. The *hadith* constitutes the major source of guidance for Muslims apart from the *Quran*.

Let us begin our reflection on the names of God by pondering some of the ninety-nine names found in the Islamic tradition. Below are twenty-five of those names. I suggest you read these names slowly, aloud, and pausing after each one. In other words, rather than just reading the names, *pray* the names:

Be ness í cent

The Beneficent... The Merciful... The Protector... The Creator... The Subtle One.

The Appreciative... The Bestower... The Generous One... The Opener... The Most Glorious One.

The Resurrector... The Truth... The First... The Last... The Source of All Goodness.

The Protecting Friend... The Alive... The Restorer... The Lord of Majesty and Bounty... The Unique.

The Maintainer... The Wise... The Gatherer... The Everlasting... The Enricher.

Were you drawn to any of these names? If so, which one(s) and why?

Were there any names that surprised you or elicited wonder or confusion? If so, which one(s) and why?

Once when I was making my annual retreat, I wanted to reflect on the names of God. I did not have access to the list of the ninety-nine names of Allah. So, I decided to create my own list of names for God. I ended up with about seventy-five. Not all the names were original to me, of course. Some are part of our venerable Judeo-Christian tradition. Here are a few of the names for God on my list. Again, I suggest you read them slowly, aloud, and with pauses:

Sweet One... Almighty One... My Beloved... Source of all Goodness... Comfort.

Goad... Oasis... Divine Comedian... The One to Whom Everything Is Tending... Unending Patience.

Perpetual Persistence... Bread of Life... Life-Giving Water... Best Friend... Humble One.

Hiding One... Revealing One... Unending Movement... Primeval Flow... Divine Tuning Fork.

Breast of My First Nourishment... Grandma/
Grandpa... Wise Farmer... Bridge Builder... Pathfinder.
Lifelong Traveling Companion... First Responder...
My Ageless Playmate... Impenetrable Mystery.
Lifeguard... Healer... My Primary Care Giver...
Home.

With each name, I asked these two questions: If this is God, then who am I? If this is God, then how do I live my life?

If God is First Responder, for example, that implies I may find myself in serious need at times. If so, I must "call" God when I am in trouble. If God is First Responder, then how do I live my life? It means I stay in touch with God always—especially through daily prayer. It also means I entrust myself to God's direction and care. And finally, it means I live my life with less fear, knowing God will be the first one to help me in my every distress.

I posted some of my names of God on my blog, "Sunflower Seeds," at melanniesvobodasnd.org. Many of my readers responded. A few responded to specific names on my list. One reacted to First Responder, writing, "I have many first responders in my family, but I never thought of God that way. It reminded me that maybe that's because I don't let God be that for me. I take charge too soon." Another was drawn to God as Ageless Playmate. She kept coming back to that name and concluded, "That name is asking me to play!"

Other readers shared some of their own favorite names of God: Mercy... Harbor... Daddy... Awesome One... Divine Intervener... Water... Peace... Sunrise. Whatever names we use when we speak to or about God, we realize that no single name can fully represent who God is. St. Gregory of Nyssa, a fourth-century bishop, wrote these wise words: "God's name is not known; it is wondered at."

Questions for Reflection

1. Are you drawn to any of the names of God in this chapter? If so, which one(s) and why?

2. What are some of your favorite names for God?

3. By what names does God call you?

Love Poem to God

If all I ever heard was the chirping of a single robin,
if all I ever smelled was the scent of one sprig of lilac,
if all I ever tasted was the sweetness of one strawberry,
if all I ever touched was the softness of a bunny's ear,
if all I ever saw was the vastness of a single starry night,
I would have reason enough
to fall helplessly in love
with Thee, my Creating God.

Digital Connection

Suggested YouTube video: "Blessed Be Your Name" by Matt Redman

CHAPTER 9

Can Beauty Help Us to Be Good?

"Beauty will save the world."

FYODOR DOSTOEVSKY'S *THE IDIOT*

E arlier we saw that beauty can charm us, heal us, and unite us. But can beauty also help us to be good? Can it help us to be moral? My short answer to that question is yes, it can. This yes comes from my personal experience and from what others have said about this question.

First, my personal experience. When I saw a theater production of *Lion King*, I had a somewhat unusual response, which began with the opening scene. The music and singing began, and one by one, all the actors dressed in magnificent animal costumes began to enter the theater—from all sides—dancing slowly down the aisles toward the stage: lions, cheetahs, antelopes, monkeys, giraffes, birds, and even a gigantic elephant. The music, the singing, the costumes, the dancing, the color—almost overwhelmed me. In fact, I got tears in my eyes. I whispered to my friend, "This is soooo beautiful!" And my very next interior thought was something like this, "I wanna be a better person." Now where did that come from? I wondered.

I had a similar feeling after seeing the movie *Schindler's List*. This film, about the Holocaust, is certainly not a pretty picture. Rather, it graphically depicts Nazi atrocities of all kinds: terror, brutality, torture, starvation, mass gassings, genocide. Yet by the end, all I could focus on was the beauty of the main character, Oskar Schindler. He was an ordinary and imperfect human being, yet he risked everything to save 1,200 Jews from certain death. I wondered, "Where did he get such courage—and love?" Later I reflected on some of the injustices of my own time and place, and I thought, "What am I doing about these?"

The Swiss theologian Hans Urs von Balthasar wrote extensively on beauty and morality. He has put into words what I believe I felt at that play and movie. Beauty, he said, has the power to stun us. It can put us into "*aesthetic arrest*." He explained why. On the deepest level of our beings, he said, we are beautiful. Therefore, we resonate sympathetically with beauty. He described that resonance as a *vibration sympathetique*. Ronald Rolheiser, OMI, explains our resonance with beauty in these words: "In the depth of our souls we carry an icon of the One who is Beautiful. We have within us the image and likeness of God, the source of all beauty." He concludes, "Beauty rouses dormant divinity within us. It stirs the soul where it is most tender."

Over the centuries, other writers have expressed this affinity between beauty and morality. The poet Rumi, a thirteenth-century Persian poet and Islamic scholar, wrote, "Let the beauty we love be what we do." In the twentieth century, British writer Evelyn Underhill said, "Beauty is the only thing really worth having....It is, after all, the visual side of goodness." And closer to our own time, Rev. Sean Parker Dennison said, "The ability to see beauty is the beginning of our moral sensibility."

This innate resonance with beauty must be nurtured in us. If it is not, then we risk dulling our moral sensibility. If we do not allow experiences of beauty to arouse the beauty and tenderness within us, we can more easily succumb to evil. We must also remember that appreciating various art forms does not automatically make us moral people. As we know, some of the Nazis who listened to classical music in the evening were the same people who committed unspeakable acts during the day.

We can view social injustice, then, as a lack of beauty or as beauty deformed. Let's take the injustice of discrimination. If we discriminate against a certain group of people, we are failing to recognize the unique beauty of those individuals. Instead, we have lumped these individuals together as "them," usually with a negative connotation. Racism, sexism, ageism, anti-Semitism, homophobia, and xenophobia are all prejudices that can lead to discriminatory acts—from the enactment of unjust laws to actual physical violence.

Jesus was in touch with his own beauty and goodness. Three times in the gospels, he hears these words from Heaven: "This is my beloved son." Jesus knew his ultimate goodness lay in his relationship with the Father, with Abba. He never forgot this. During his lifetime, Jesus nurtured the tenderness within him by his attention to beauty—the beauty of bread rising, wine fermenting, relaxing with friends, praying alone on a mountain. He spoke of the beauty of compassion, parental love, forgiveness. Because Jesus saw people as individuals, he did not succumb to the prejudices that many others held. For example, he saw women as individuals and seemed to enjoy their company and value their experience. He befriended Gentiles. He praised a centurion, a member of the occupational force. And he made a Samaritan the surprising hero in one of his parables.

In the end, Jesus himself was subjected to ugliness of all kinds. He was arrested under the cover of darkness. He was unjustly tried. He was abused and tortured by the Roman soldiers. He was wrongfully sentenced to die. He was subjected to a slow and agonizing death. The image of Jesus on the cross is, in one sense, an ugly icon. But if we look beneath the surface, we get a glimpse of the beauty of Jesus' incredible love, faith, courage, and forgiveness.

I began this chapter with the frequently quoted words of Dostoevsky, "Beauty will save the world." The words are uttered by Prince Myskin in Dostoevsky's novel *The Idiot*. When the Prince is asked, *which* beauty will save the world? He responds, "*Who* will save the world?" Then he adds, "If beauty will save the world, it will be a *person*." We Christians believe that person is Jesus. We also believe we have the privilege of partnering with this beautiful Jesus in bringing salvation to our world.

Questions for Reflection

1. Have you ever had an experience of beauty that stunned you, moved you to tears, or made you want to be a better person? If so, reflect on that experience and try to put into words your response to the beauty you experienced.

2. Who or what helps you to stay in touch with your own goodness? How do you help others to stay in touch with their own goodness?

3. Identify one of your prejudices. What step might you take to begin to "reduce" this prejudice?

Below are a few quotations about beauty and our moral sense. I suggest you read these slowly and see if you agree or disagree with any of them.

1. "Beauty is a bridge to justice. If in this millennium we really want justice, we must learn to cultivate beauty."
   ■ **JOAN CHITTISTER, OSB**

2. "We need beauty because it makes us ache to be worthy of it." ■ **MARY OLIVER**

3. "In such ugly times, the only protest is beauty."
   ■ **PHIL OCHS**

4. "In the face of brutality, what's needed is tenderness; in the face of hype and ideology, what's needed is truth; in the face of bitterness and curses, what's needed are graciousness and blessing; in the face of hatred and murder, what's needed are love and forgiveness; and, in the face of all the ugliness and vulgarity that so pervades our world and the evening news, what's needed is beauty."
   ■ **RONALD ROLHEISER, OMI**

5. "An apparent enthusiasm for the beautiful is mere idle talk when divorced from the sense of a divine summons to change one's life." ■ **HANS URS VON BALTHASAR**

6. "Beauty is a matter not simply of harmony and proportion...but of ethical transcendence, the capacity to share in the pathos of another." ■ **PETER C. HODGSON**

7. "Beauty draws us to God, its ultimate source, more effectively than preaching or proselytizing."

   ■ **GAIL PORTER**

8. "Beauty awakens the soul to act."

   ■ **DANTE ALIGHIERI**

9. "Sometimes people are beautiful.
   Not in looks.
   Not in what they say.
   Just in what they are."

   ■ **MARKUS ZUSACK**

10. "There is nothing more beautiful than when someone goes out of their way to make life beautiful for others."

    ■ **MANDY HALE**

Digital Connection

Suggested YouTube video: "Room at the Table"
by Carrie Newcomer (with lyrics)

CHAPTER 10

Reverencing the Ordinary

*"Extraordinary magic is woven
through ordinary life. Look around!"*

AMY LEIGH MERCREE

It is relatively easy to appreciate beauty that is extraordinary: the birth of a baby, a solar eclipse, the Grand Canyon, a whale breaching, a glacier calving, a hillside covered with hundreds of red tulips. But can we also appreciate the ordinary beauty in our everyday life: a glass of water, the softness of a kitten's fur, the rain forming puddles in the driveway, a loved one's voice, the slant of light coming through the window? Can we even *reverence* these *ordinary* things?

What does it mean to reverence something? The word *reverence* comes from the Latin *revereri*, which means *to stand in awe*. Synonyms we most often use today are *respect, esteem, regard*. The word can also refer to gestures that express esteem such as a bow or a curtsey. To reverence the ordinary means, then, to respect and have esteem for the everyday and the commonplace. (Maybe we should bow to our cup of coffee in the morning or curtsey to our cat!)

The fact is, most of our life is composed of the ordinary. This means if we fail to find beauty there, we miss out on a lot of beauty! Omid Safi, a professor of Islamic studies at Duke University, wrote an article about the spirituality of the ordinary. In it he quotes Rabbi Abraham Heschel, who said, "Wonder or radical amazement is the chief characteristic of the religious [person's] attitude toward history and nature." We might ask, is wonder or radical amazement part of *our* attitude toward the ordinary?

Safi continues, "God and the sacred, the enchanted and the luminous, are not 'over there' somewhere. They are right here, where we are." He concludes, "Seeking awe in the ordinary...is the beginning of the spiritual life."

When directing retreats, I often suggest this exercise to help retreatants "seek awe in the ordinary." I ask them to dialogue with something ordinary. They can choose some living natural entity, such as a plant or animal. Or a nonliving thing, such as a rock, a pond, or the sun. Or they can also select a human-made object, such as a vase or a rocking chair. I tell them: "Just *be* with the object; then, *observe* everything you can about the object; then, *ask* the object to share some of its wisdom with you; and finally, *listen*."

At first, we might feel pretty silly talking to an orange, a tree, or a squirrel. And chances are we will not actually hear with our ears the object speaking. But if we are patient, we just might hear the object with our heart. Sometimes a remarkable revelation might occur. I encourage my retreatants to write down their dialogue. This helps to slow the process.

My retreatants have dialogued with the sun, moon, wind, stars, and ocean. They have conversed with the rain, a single blade of grass, a seagull, an apple, a staircase, a door, a butterfly, a mailbox, a feather, a pine tree, a telephone pole, a wastebasket, and much more.

Here are a few examples. One retreatant in Pennsylvania heard an old tree say to her, "Be deeply rooted...branch out with love... wave often." Another retreatant in New Jersey found a seagull feather and said to it, "You must feel so close to God when you fly." But the feather replied, "You don't have to fly to be close to God. Just *be* in the silence, and God will come and greet you." In Kansas, one retreatant heard a blade of grass say, "I love it when children play, wrestle, and romp on me...or when I'm used for a ballgame or for spreading out a picnic lunch....I just love being a part of God's beautiful world. I just love being me!" A retreatant in Illinois received this wisdom from a gentle breeze: "Be gentle with everyone. You never know what heaviness they might be bearing. At a time like that, they don't need my cousin, the whirlwind. Be a gentle breeze for them through your words, actions, and attitudes." A peach in Alabama told one retreatant: "Slow down. All things will ripen in their time. Ripening can't be hurried. Savor life. Don't waste all the little pleasures God gave us to enjoy."

To encourage you to try this exercise, I have written a longer dialogue that I had with something ordinary: the fire hydrant in front of our convent:

Hi, Mr. Fire Hydrant. How are you today?

* Same as ever, I guess.

I almost didn't notice you standing on our tree lawn.

* Few people do.

But you're bright red. How could I walk by you almost every day on my way to church and not notice you?

* Because I'm always here, that's how. We tend to overlook things that are always there. Like trees. Like buildings. Like people even.

That's true, sadly.

* I'll tell you who notices me. Firefighters. I bet they know exact-

ly where all of us hydrants are in this town. And I've heard that a fire hydrant in front of your house can make your house more attractive to potential buyers. I guess we exude a sense of safety and security.

I see. Do you have a name?

* My friends call me Sentinel.

Sentinel. How beautiful—and appropriate.

* Thank you. What's your name?

Melannie.

* Melannie. What a cutesy and upbeat name.

Tell me, Sentinel, what's it like being a fire hydrant?

*Well, sometimes it's not easy. Dogs use me for you-know-what. And birds sit on my head and do their you-know-what on me too.

I'm sorry about that. (I notice a little birdie poop on his head.)

* That's okay. Everyone should be able to take a little you-know-what every now and then. It's a part of life.

Do you have any other piece of wisdom you can share with me?

* Well, as you can see, I am not very attractive.

Oh, don't say that!

* But it's true! If someone said you looked like a fire hydrant, would you be complimented?

Well... well...

* See? Self-knowledge and self-acceptance are very important. And despite my chunky looks, I am very valuable. When this valve is opened, a surge of water will come out to help put out a fire. Years ago, I helped put out a fire on a lady's front porch down the street a bit. Afterward, she ran to me and gave me a big hug. That was the first and only hug I ever received. It was... it was quite wonderful...

I'm sure it was. I notice there's a long metal pole sticking straight up on you. Is that because of all the snow we get?

* That's right. In winter I can get buried beneath all that lake-effect snow. If I do, this pole tells the firefighters exactly where I am.

Well, Sentinel, thank you for talking to me. I will never take you for granted again. And thank you for your service to our community.

* You're welcome, Melannie.

(I take leave of Sentinel. But before I do, I check to see it anyone is looking. No one is. So, I bend over and give Sentinel a quick firm hug. And as I do, I feel his metal body soften—just a little.)

Questions for Reflection

1. Do you usually take ordinary things for granted or do you reverence and appreciate them? If possible, give a few examples of ordinary things you tend to take for granted and those you tend to reverence and appreciate. What makes the difference?

2. Have you ever experienced something ordinary as luminous, that is, as dazzling or revelatory?

3. If you do the exercise suggested in this chapter, then reflect on these questions: What object did you choose to dialogue with? What did you learn? Did this activity alter your perception of the object in any way? If so, how?

Today Was a Very Good Day

Today was a very good day.
In fact, it was a beautiful day!
It was a wonderful, enchanting,
remarkable, miraculous day.
What's more,
nothing out of the ordinary
happened.

Digital Connection

Suggested YouTube video: "Ordinary Miracle"
by Sarah McLachlan (song with lyrics by Ti Na)

CHAPTER 11

The Beauty of Movement

"God is the movement in the direction of home."

MARTIN BUBER

We are moving.

Even when we are sitting in a comfortable chair or lying in bed, we are moving. More accurately, we are zooming! As I sit here writing this book and as you sit there reading it, the earth is rotating 1,040 miles per hour—and it is taking all of us along for the ride. We do not feel this zooming, of course, because our atmosphere is zooming right along with us.

But we are moving even more than that. Our rotating planet is simultaneously revolving around the sun at (hang on to your hat!) 66,500 miles per hour! And that is not all. Our entire solar system is moving too. Our sun with its orbiting planets sits on the outer edges of the Milky Way, a gigantic rotating galaxy composed of 100 billion stars. For our solar system to rotate just once within this humongous galaxy takes about 250 million years!

But there is even more. Not only are all the planets and stars moving, so is every single cell in our bodies! Every cell that composes our brain, heart, liver, small intestine, femurs, eyes, fingertips—all are moving! And so is every single atom that composes every single mountain, rock, tree, raindrop, whale, beetle, blueberry, and flamingo feather. Everything is moving. Every thing. Movement and not fixedness lies at the heart of our universe.

Why is it important to remember this basic and beautiful truth? Because creation reflects the Creator. For too long, humankind thought of God as a person "up there" or "out there." Aristotle conceived of God as the Unmoved Mover. In other words, as the Perfectly Changeless One. But throughout history there have been individuals who thought of God in more dynamic terms. Even St. Thomas Aquinas, who described God as the Prime Mover, also said God was Pure Act. St. Bonaventure conceived of God as Diffusive Love. That means God was not merely Love. God was *Loving*—diffusively. A great medieval mystic, Mechthild of Magdeburg, wrote about the "restless Godhead," an "overflow...which never stands still and always flows effortlessly and without ceasing." Contemporary theologian Elizabeth Johnson says there is no place in the universe and in human hearts where God is not "drawing near and passing by." God is forever moving.

Steven Bevans, SVD, of the Catholic Theological Union, has written an essay titled "God Is a Verb." In it he says, "I've begun to think of God as a Movement, an Embrace, a Flow—moving through the cosmos and history, embracing wounded and suffering creation, flowing through the smallest subatomic particle as well as complex organisms." He pictures all of creation engaged in a cosmic dance that God is leading. He imagines a dance like the *conga* where one person leads and everyone else forms a line behind the leader, hanging on to each other's waist as they weave around the dance hall to a vibrant Latin rhythm. God as First Dancer, Lead

Dancer, Eternal Dancer! Such an image of God can shape the way we view the universe, as well as the way we live and work and play with one another.

If movement lies at the core of all that is, then why do we humans struggle so much with the movement we call change? Why do we so often resist change or even rail against it? This interpretation of Original Sin might aid our understanding. Some theologians have described Original Sin as *inertia*. They maintain that Original Sin is the basic human tendency to want to stay put, to keep things as they are, to not rock the boat. Yet inertia is incompatible with all those qualities necessary to live our Christian life with faith and vigor. What qualities? Vocation... conversion... discipleship... letting go... service... forgiveness... love. These qualities presume movement and change.

There is an incident in the Second Book of Samuel that suggests God likes to move (2 Sam 7:1–7). It occurs when David is finally settled in his new palace. One day he gets what he thinks is a great idea: "I will build a house for God." He shares his idea with the prophet Samuel, who also thinks it is a good idea. But that night, Samuel is visited by God, who strongly rejects David's plans. He says (in essence), "I have dwelt in a tent since the day I led you out of Egypt. I don't want a house!" God's reaction, some Scripture scholars say, shows that God prefers the freedom and mobility that tent dwelling gives rather than the confinement and fixedness that a house would give. Some raise the question, "By putting God into a house, is David trying to confine and control God?"

Jesus moved. His whole life was a movement from Bethlehem and Nazareth to the city of Jerusalem. As a young boy, he "*advanced* in wisdom and age," Luke tells us. Advancing implies movement. During his public ministry, Jesus was always on the go, walking from village to village on foot. When he encounters the sick, he is *moved with compassion*. When he loses his friend Lazarus to death, Jesus is *moved to tears*. His interior growth and understanding were always advancing too, as he gradually learned to follow the dance steps the Spirit was teaching him. At times, his disciples tried to curb his movement. At the transfiguration, Peter, wanted to stay put on the beautiful mountaintop. "I will make three tents here," he says to Jesus. But Jesus refused to stay put there—or anywhere. Instead, he led his disciples down from Tabor as he moved ever closer to Jerusalem, to death, and to resurrection.

Movement and change can be beautiful, for it is through them we become the persons God is calling us to be. Through movement and change, we are joining the great and beautiful cosmic dance—the dance by which Jesus is leading all creation home.

Questions for Reflection

1. Does the movement inherent in the cosmos influence your concept of God? If so, how? If not, why not?

2. Do you ordinarily resist change or welcome change in your life? Why?

3. Do you ever dance for God or with God? For example, have you ever danced your prayer?

Prayer to a Dancing God

Oh, Dancing God,
you invite all creation to join you
in the one, grand Cosmic Dance.
The sun and planets dance with each other,
the stars and galaxies are dancing too.
Every atom is dancing with other atoms,
forming molecules that dance themselves
into raindrops and flowers, earthworms and otters,
pandas and parakeets, emus and elephants,
and me.
Teach me to dance my life away, Dancer God.
Be my partner. Take the lead.
Teach me how to step and glide, pause and rise,
bend and twist and twirl—all
to the rhythms of your beautiful creation,
to the beatings of my own heart,
and to the gentle urgings of your Swirling Spirit.
I ask for these graces through Jesus,
who stepped into our world at Bethlehem,
danced at the wedding feast of Cana,
moved through the streets of Palestine,
all the way to Calvary.
And, on Easter Sunday morning,
this same Jesus sprang out of the darkness of the tomb,
swaying, skipping, whirling, twirling
into the brightness of everlasting life. Amen.

Digital Connection

Suggested YouTube video: "Where the Hell Is Matt?" (2012 version)

CHAPTER 12

The Beauty of Familiar Things

"When it comes to life, the critical thing is whether you take things for granted or take them with gratitude."

G.K. CHESTERTON

"Familiarity breeds contempt," says the old adage. That might be an exaggeration. Yet familiarity can dull our appreciation of beauty. If we see the same beauty over and over again, we can begin to take it for granted. Worse yet, we can reach a point where we do not even notice it anymore.

Several years ago, some of my relatives from the Czech Republic were visiting. I decided to drive them into Cleveland for the day. We were heading toward the city on the Shoreway, which, at one point, suddenly opens up onto Lake Erie. When my relatives caught sight of that vast expanse of water, they gasped. As we continued along the shore, they kept pointing out the beauty they saw: the waves crashing against the break wall, the large ships on the horizon, and the hundreds of noisy seagulls flying in circles above the water. My cousin Eva reminded me that the Czech Republic was a landlocked country. Hence their excitement. Now, I had made that drive thousands of times into Cleveland, and I always enjoyed seeing Lake Erie. But the reaction of my relatives gave me a greater appreciation of the beauty of this familiar but remarkable body of water.

Familiarity is not the only thing that can lesson our appreciation of beauty. So can cynicism. Cynics are individuals who think the worst about other people and, by extension, life itself. Cynics are disenchanted with life. Their mantras include, "A better world is not possible....People are inherently selfish and lazy....It's the same old same old....What's the use of trying to make things better? Nothing helps."

If we say, for example, "Look at that gorgeous sunset!" The cynic says, "It's caused by pollution, you know."

If we say, "That couple has been married for over fifty years! Isn't that wonderful?" The cynic says, "I bet they've had a heck of a lot of fights!"

If we say, "I think most parents really take good care of their children." The cynic says, "Isn't that their job?"

If we say, "Aren't our national parks beautiful?" The cynic says, "If you ask me, the parks are a waste of space. We should be doing something constructive with all that land."

Familiarity and cynicism can dull even the beauty and impact of sacred Scripture. When we hear those familiar opening words of the parable of the prodigal son, "A man had two sons," do we ever think, "I've heard this story a million times," so we stop listening?

Or if we hear, "Love one another," do we ever think, "Easier said than done," and stop there?

Or when we hear, "Take up your cross," do we ever think, "I

don't like this Scripture passage. It's too negative."

How can we prevent familiarity or cynicism from dulling our sense of beauty? Here are three small practices that can help.

First, *look deeper*. If we would put pictures of a swamp and a golf course side by side and ask people, "Which one is more beautiful?" chances are many people would pick the golf course with its manicured lawns, perfectly groomed bushes, and strategically placed trees. That golf course, however, might be using dangerous pesticides to produce such beauty. And what about the swamp? Swamps are ugly, right? Has not the very word *swamp* come to mean a place filled with corruption? But, if we look deeper, we will see that swamps are actually beautiful. In fact, they are vital for a healthy ecosystem. Swamps or wetlands prevent flooding by absorbing excess water, much like a sponge. They also filter and purify surface water and provide habitats for a host of fish and other wildlife. Swamps or wetlands are beautiful!

If we look deeper, we will see beauty in creatures often labeled ugly—such as hyenas and bats. Hyenas are beautiful because they play a significant role in nature's "garbage patrol." By dining on carcasses, they help prevent the spread of disease. Similarly, a single bat eats about 7,000 insects per night—most of them mosquitos. By doing this, bats not only defend against mosquito-borne diseases but also make your backyard a more pleasant place to relax. George Washington Carver, the American agricultural scientist and inventor, said, "Anything will give up its secrets if you love it enough." Could we not also say, "Anything will reveal its *beauty* if you *look deeply* and love it enough"?

A second way to keep our sense of beauty alive is this: *Look, hear, smell, taste, and touch things as if you were experiencing them for the FIRST time*. If this were the first time you saw a tree, what would you think? How would you feel? If this were the first time you experienced snow, what would you think or do? As someone suggested, if you really want to see or experience the world, go for a walk with a child. For most little children *are* experiencing the world for the first time, so they are fascinated by things we adults often take for granted.

That reminds me of a little story. A woman, living on the shores of Lake Huron, had her three-year-old grandson visiting for Christmas. One morning the two of them sat in the living room and watched the sunrise over the lake. It was a beautiful sight, with the yellow and orange light reflecting on the water. The next morning the woman was in the kitchen working when she heard her grandson yelling excitedly from the living room, "Grandma! Come quick! It's doing it again!"

A third way to appreciate beauty is to *look, hear, touch, smell, and taste things as if it were for the LAST time*. If this were the last time you were seeing the face of a loved one, what would you want to remember? If this were the last orange you would ever eat, how would you eat it—slowly? Even reverently? If this were the last night you would be able to see the stars, would you take the trouble to go outside after dark—despite the chill in the air—to gaze upon them? And finally, if today were the last day of your life, how would you live it?

Questions for Reflection

1. Can you name something you once took for granted but now you don't? What caused the change in your attitude?

2. Has a little child ever made you appreciate something you were taking for granted? Recall the incident and your feelings before, during, and after the incident.

3. Select something or someone you are taking for granted. Try looking deeper. Or look at this object or person as if for the first or last time. Was your attitude toward the object or person changed at all by doing this?

Thank You, God, for Familiar Things

Thank you, God, for familiar things.
For old bedroom slippers, so comfy on our feet,
offering ample space for bunions and each individual toe.
Thank you for soft living room chairs,
that welcome every plop or flop of ours,
inviting us to relax awhile at the end of a long day.
Thank you, God, for our late-model car
with its specific quirks we are long accustomed to,
(that same car accustomed to our quirks too!)
Thank you for old dogs who, even after all these years,
still greet us with their tails wagging
as if we were someone new and fresh.

Thank you, God, for familiar Scripture verses
that tell us unceasingly of your unceasing love for us,
and for the sacred rituals we partake in,

and sometimes dare to yawn or doze through.
Thank you for the familiar people in our lives
who are always near or a phone call away,
until they aren't.

Thank you, God, for familiar things—
the usual, the ordinary, the everyday—
all those things we so often take for granted
without taking the time to offer you
a good and proper "Thank You." Amen.

Digital Connection

Suggested YouTube: "Holy Now" (with lyrics and captions)
by Peter Mayer.

CHAPTER 13

Beautiful Jesus

"The message of Christ is not Christianity.
The message of Christianity is Christ."

GARY AMIRAULT

Jesus was a beautiful person. Trace his steps in the gospel and, chances are, you too will be drawn to this beautiful man from Galilee.

Hear his essential teachings: love one another, forgive, pray, share, give, care for those in need, fear not, have courage, trust, God is in your midst, take up your cross, follow me, I call you friends, I am with you until the end of time.

See him interact with people. See him playing with little children, touching lepers, conversing with men and women, making time for his friends, enjoying good food and wine, listening attentively to people's stories, holding his own with learned scholars. See him being amazed at the love of a soldier for his servant, at the spunk of a Gentile woman who would not take "no" for an answer, at the generosity of an elderly widow who, in giving two small coins, gave her all.

See him dancing at a wedding in Cana. See him working his

first miracle there at his mother's request—not to restore a life, not to eradicate excruciating pain. No, working a miracle to save the young couple and their families from embarrassment, a miracle to extend the guests' pleasure by making the party last a little longer.

See Jesus pray... alone on a hilltop in the early hours of the morning... with his closest friends... with those gathered in the synagogue for worship... See him pray on ordinary days... on the Sabbath... while celebrating the Passover with his friends for the last time... and in an olive garden right before his arrest, unjust trial, torture, and horrific death.

Hear Jesus at prayer addressing the Almighty, Everlasting, All-knowing God as Abba, Father.

See him earlier at age twelve, sitting in the Temple in Jerusalem, engaging in discussions with religious leaders many times his age... See him humbly obeying his parents... and see him growing in wisdom. See Jesus learning the carpentry trade from Joseph... fashioning tables, chairs, doorframes, cradles, yokes... Be with him in the desert as his ponders the meaning and purpose of life... as he considers what to do with his life... as he undergoes a profound religious experience, clarifying his divine call... as he leaves the security and familiarity of family and friends and takes to the open road—by foot—to speak words that must be spoken and to perform deeds that must be done.

See Jesus smiling at the cuteness and unpredictability of children. See him laughing at dinner with his friends. And see Jesus weeping when he is told of the death of John the Baptist. See him weeping outside the tomb of his good friend Lazarus. See him weeping as he gazes down on the doomed city of Jerusalem teeming with people, *his* people. Hear him compare himself to a good shepherd, to a mother hen, to a grape vine that carries nourishment to every single branch, to living water, to light, to the bread of life.

Hear Jesus challenging his disciples and the crowds, to welcome the stranger, the refugee, to care for the widow and the orphan, to nurse the sick, feed the hungry, clothe the naked, visit the imprisoned, to forgive again and again and again, to pray always, and to trust in God's unconditional love.

See Jesus angry, angry at the money changers who defiled the Temple and cheated the poor, angry at certain Pharisees who clung to the husk of the law while ignoring the nutritious fruit within, angry that what should not be, was, and what should be, was not.

Hear him speak of the beauty and mystery of life, the potential in a lowly mustard seed, the value of a single sheep, the ingratitude of a younger son, his eventual repentance and return, the anger of his older brother, and the incredible father whose love was as wide as the sea and expansive enough to embrace both of his sons. Hear him speak of the amazing compassion of a Samaritan—someone usually thought of as an enemy. Hear him muse on the recurrence of the changing seasons, parents' concern for their children, the healthy balance of fasting and feasting, the inevitability of death, the miracle of rebirth.

Yes, you may be thinking. But did not this beautiful Jesus suffer an ugly end? Was he not brutally beaten and tortured and put to death? Yes, he was. But look beneath the ugliness of his crucifixion and see his absolute trust in Abba... his amazing courage... his complete surrender... his incredible love for humanity—for us. For you and me. And look beyond his death to the empty tomb... to his glorious resurrection—a resurrection not solely his but ours as well. For, in living and dying and rising, this beautiful Jesus draws all of us to follow in his Way, a Way that leads to beauty unimaginable, joy immeasurable, and life everlasting.

Questions for Reflection

1. What aspect of Jesus' beauty touches you the most? Why?

2. In what other way(s) was Jesus beautiful?

3. How are you trying to follow in the way of Jesus?

The Incarnation

And the Word became flesh.
What does that mean?
It means God in carnus,
conceived in a woman, implanted in a womb.
It means gestation and gradual growth.
It means composed of the basic elements of the cosmos.
It means embedded within earth's community of beings.
It means a unique DNA...
and muscles, lipids, neurons, blood, bone.
It means a brain, lungs, a digestive tract, a beating heart.
It means being born of a woman, a mother, Mary.
And the Word became flesh.
It means the Divine became human,
the Eternal entered time,
the Omnipresent submitted to the confines of specific places.
The Beyond-the-Beyond was now here, now now.
The Almighty became weak, vulnerable, helpless.
Sovereignty was transformed into lowliness.
The Thundering Voice on Sinai, now an infant's whimper,
now a piercing Waah!

The Self-Existent One, now a suckling at a mother's breast.
The Always Was, now part of the ever-changing is.
The Ancient of Days, now a newborn.
The Totally Other, now one of us.
The Transcendent One, now Emmanuel.
God-with-us, God-for-us, God-among-us, Jesus.
Then and now. There and here. Yesterday. Today. Tomorrow.

And what is our response to this event ungraspable?
A breathless, "Wow!" Then a whispered,
"Thank you... Thank you!"

Digital Connection

Suggested YouTube video: "The Gentle Healer"
by Michael Card (Champion Studios)

CHAPTER 14

The Beauty of Me

"God thinks I am a good idea."

JAN JOHNSON

My years of ministering in education, formation, and spiritual direction have led me to this conclusion: much of the world's evil stems from people, like you and me, not being aware of our own beauty. I am convinced, if we did recognize our intrinsic beauty, we would be less inclined to do ugly things and more drawn to do beautiful things.

Recognizing our own beauty begins, however, with acknowledging that we are both saint and sinner. We are capable of doing great good, yes. At the same time, we are capable of doing great evil. If we forget either of these aspects of our selfhood, we are in serious trouble.

Jesus told a parable about a man who forgot he was a sinner (Lk 18:9–14). In the parable of the Pharisee and the tax collector, the Pharisee comes to the Temple to pray. He struts right up to the front and begins by thanking God that he is "not like the rest of humanity—greedy, dishonest, adulterous." He is grateful he is not like the tax collector who is also praying in the temple. Then the Pharisee recites a list of all his good deeds and religious practices. In his praying, however, the Pharisee is blind to the ugly sin of his self-righteousness. In sharp contrast is the tax collector. He is fully aware of his sinfulness— so much so, he hangs his head, beats his breast, and prays, "O God, be merciful to me a sinner." The parable reminds us that when we deny our capacity for sin, we are denying a part of who we are.

But (and that is a major but) our sinfulness is only *part* of who we are. We are also good and beautiful! More often than not, we dwell on our shortcomings rather than our goodness. Writer Macrina Wiederkehr, OSB, has suggested that, before crawling into bed at night, we should pray, "Dear God, please tell me the whole truth about myself—no matter how wonderful it is!" I smiled when I first read those words. Why? Because I had assumed the prayer would be, "Dear God, please tell me the whole truth about myself—no matter how *terrible* it is!"

I saw a video recently where several women were chosen to participate in an experiment. One by one they were taken to a spacious room where a man sat with a drawing board behind a curtain. He was a forensic sketch artist. He and each participant could not see each other. The forensic artist asked each woman to describe herself. "Tell me about your hair," he began. The women described their hair and then their facial features. One woman said, "My mother always said I had a big chin." Others said things like, "I have a fat face... a protruding jaw... too many freckles." Next, each woman was paired up with another person, a stranger, for several minutes. When each woman returned to the room, she was asked to describe the other person she had just met. Once again, the forensic artist drew the person being described: "She had a cute nose... a friendly, open face... her eyes lit up when she spoke."

Then the two sketches of the same woman were placed side by

side. The results were amazing. The sketch of the woman's self-description was noticeably less flattering than the one based on the stranger's description. Furthermore, in all cases, the sketch of the stranger's description was more accurate! When the women saw both sketches of themselves, some of them were emotionally moved—nearly to tears. One said, "We're always analyzing and trying to fix what's not right with ourselves, instead of appreciating all the things that are right." Her words apply to more than our *external features*. They apply to our *inner self* as well.

Sometimes our religious education and formation overemphasized our sinfulness to the detriment of our beauty. Most of us who entered religious life in the 1960s, for example, could never forget we were sinners, for many religious practices of that era reinforced our failings. We performed acts of humility to curb our pride. We beat ourselves with small cords to control our unruly body. We publicly confessed our faults weekly and asked for a penance. What faults? "I broke a cup. I broke silence. I spilled a pitcher of milk. I did not pray the three o'clock prayer twice. I failed to do my housework once." The list of our failings was long. (Our actual sins we saved for the confessional.) Reciting our many failings each week tended to blind us to our beauty and goodness.

I wondered, even back then, what if we had publicly "confessed" our goodness every week instead of our failings? What if we had said things like this: "I prayed every day. I was basically kind. I studied hard for my classes. I laughed a lot. I deeply desire to help other people. I want to give my whole life to God." Reciting such a list might have been considered boastful maybe, but it would have been an acknowledgment of our basic goodness.

The writer and retreat director Edwina Gateley says this: "Only a few people believe themselves beautiful. That saddens me: it is a diminishment of the human potential for grace and excellence."

She is implying that a healthy awareness of our own beauty increases our potential for goodness. Gateley adds, "When we diminish ourselves, we diminish God."

How might we grow in appreciation of our own beauty? First, we can remember that we are created by God. In his letter to the Ephesians, St. Paul writes, "For we are God's handiwork" (Eph 2:10). Other translations say, "We are God's masterpiece" or "We are God's work of art." Second, we can remember that we are redeemed by Jesus. In the gospels, Jesus calls his disciples (and us!) by many endearing terms: "little ones, children, little flock, beloved, companions, friends." Jesus sees so much beauty in us that he freely gave his life for us on Calvary. If Jesus sees us as beautiful and worthy of his love, should we not see ourselves as beautiful and lovable?

A third way to grow in appreciation of our beauty is to pay more attention to the positive feedback we get on an ordinary day—the smiles, thank yous, little compliments, and messages from friends. We might even want to take time in prayer to list some of the things we are doing right in our life or some specific signs of our goodness—such as, "I pray regularly (I even read books like this one!), I care for my family, I try to help those in need, I am responsible, I am honest." And the list goes on. And finally, in humility and truth, we might even try writing a prayer of thanksgiving for "the beauty of me."

Questions for Reflection

1. What individuals in your life have made you aware of your own goodness and beauty? How did they do this?

2. What are some of the ways you try to help others appreciate their goodness and beauty?

3. This chapter gives a few ways we can grow in appreciation of our own beauty. Are there other ways you can add?

A Prayer of Thanksgiving for the Beauty of Me

Thank you, God, for the beauty of me,
for the strand of DNA that is uniquely mine,
for the carbon, oxygen, and other elements
my body is borrowing for my sojourn here on earth.
Thank you for all my ancestors
who contributed to making me me.
Thank you for the beauty of this amazing world.
I am honored to be a part of it.
Thank you for my past experiences
that have helped form the me I am today:
the wins and losses, joy and pain.
Thank you for all the beautiful people
I meet and interact with every day.

Thank you, God, for my particular gift of prayer,
for my deep desire to do good,
for my profound yearning for you.

Thank you, God, for my unique and precious life.
Thank you, God, for the beauty of me. Amen.

Digital Connection

Suggested music video: "Beautiful" by MercyMe
(with lyrics by thelindazoo)

CHAPTER 15

The Beauty of Prayer

"To pray is to laugh, whistle, dance on happy feet, sing, shout, and jump higher than ever before. But it is also to whisper, wonder, stumble in dark places, cry, scream, or just hold a tired head in tired hands and wait....Prayer is our tired reaching out to the One who holds us closer and loves us more than we would dare imagine."

GRETA SCHRUMM

What is the connection between beauty and prayer? First, beauty can elicit prayer. When I stand at a scenic overlook on the Blue Ridge Parkway, for example, and I behold the valley spread out below me, I find myself spontaneously whispering things like, "Wow, God!" or, "What an incredible artist you are!" or simply, "Thank you, God! Thank you!" The panoramic beauty has moved me to pray. So, prayer can be a response to the beauty we come upon on any given day. For, as we saw earlier, beauty is like a magnet drawing us to beauty's source.

But beauty often urges us to go beyond mere admiration. Beauty makes us want *to know* that source, that power whence the beauty comes. And as Christians, we believe that source is a *someone*, a *person* we want to know. And one way we come to know some-one—anyone—is by communicating with them, that is, by entering into dialogue with them. Prayer is the name we give to dialoging with God.

There is another connection between beauty and prayer. Simply put, prayer itself is a thing of beauty. The mere fact that we can enter into a conversation with God is itself a wondrous gift. St. John Chrysostom wrote, "What a blessing! What an honor! We are able to talk to God in prayer, to have a confidential chat with Christ!" Throughout human history, God has encouraged such a chat, such a dialogue. In fact, God initiated the conversation between God and humankind. Genesis 3 says God had the habit of conversing with Adam and Eve in the garden "at the breezy time of day." It is God once again who initiates the dialogue with Abram (Gen 12) and, later, with Moses in the burning bush (chapters 3 and 4 of Exodus). Throughout Scripture God is shown as eager to enter into a loving relationship with individuals, with the Israelite communi-ty, and with all humankind.

When we go to prayer, then, our attitude should not be, "Pardon me, God. I know you're very busy. But this will take only a minute." As if God were too preoccupied with more important matters to be bothered with us. Instead, we should imagine God as a dear friend who sees us coming and is already smiling and hastening toward us. We might even imagine God embracing us warmly and saying, "You've come! I'm so glad to see you again! I've been waiting for you. Sit down now and tell me, how *are* you? How are things going for you?" God is eager to hear our prayer. This God is with us always, yes, but in prayer we intentionally place ourselves in God's presence in order to converse directly with this Divine Person.

What else can we say about this beautiful gift called prayer? We can say that the purpose of prayer is love. As the saints and mystics keep telling us, we do not pray because we love prayer. We pray because we love God. And prayer is one of the primary ways we nourish that love relationship. Prayer, then, is not an end in itself. Prayer is only a means to an end. That end is always love—not only between God and me, but between God, me, and other people. Already in the third century, St. Cyprian, bishop and martyr of Carthage, expressed the direct link between prayer and love of others when he wrote: "It is a barren prayer that does not go hand in hand with alms." If our prayer is authentic, sooner or later it will lead us to good works, to help those in need. The evidence of good prayer, then, is not how long we pray, how many words we use, or how creative our prayer is. The evidence of good prayer is a life of love for others. Period.

The Trappist monk Thomas Merton prayed many hours a day. He also wrote a lot about prayer. One thing he warned against was turning prayer into a project—or worse, turning prayer into an onerous chore. He counseled others, "Quit trying so hard in prayer. How does an apple ripen? It just sits in the sun." Merton also stressed showing up for prayer every day. He maintained how important it was "to keep our daily appointment with mystery."

Our prayer is likely to take different forms as we journey through life. And that's fine, because there is no single best way to pray. A friend shared this quote with me recently: "Religion is sitting in church and thinking about kayaking. Spirituality is sitting in a kayak and thinking about God." I may not agree completely (we can sit in a church and think about God too!), yet, the quote does reinforce the notion that an experience of beauty—such as kayaking—can draw us to God. (Who knows? Next time you are kayaking, look around! God might be in the kayak next to you!)

And finally, our prayer will change us. Maybe that is one reason we avoid prayer at times. We have this intuitive sense that if we keep praying, God is going to ask us to change something in ourselves: our attitude, priorities, or behavior maybe. We sense that if we hang around with God in prayer, some of God's attitudes, priorities, and behaviors (as seen especially in the life and teachings of Jesus) will rub off on us. In that sense, prayer is dangerous. Writes Richard Foster, "Prayer is the central avenue God uses to transform us." Annie Dillard says we should wear crash helmets when worshiping in church. Well, maybe we should fasten our seat belts every time we pray too!

Questions for Reflection

1. Has your prayer ever been a response to beauty? If so, reflect on the beauty you experienced. What prayer did it evoke in you?

2. Reflect on your personal prayer. How do you pray? When? Where? What seems to work for you? What does not seem to work for you?

3. Do any of the quotes (in the reflection above or the ones below) touch you today? If so, which one(s)? Why?

Quotations on Prayer

1. "Is prayer your steering wheel or your spare tire?"

   ■ CORRIE TEN BOOM

2. "Prayer means learning to see the world from God's point of view." ■ RABBI ABRAHAM HESCHEL

3. "We must move from asking God to take care of the things that are breaking our hearts, to praying about the things that are breaking *God's* heart."

   ■ MARGARET GEBB

4. "Prayer is like a window. It is a way of opening our self to God." ■ JEAN GILL

5. "Without this one-hour-a-day-for-God, my life loses its coherency, and I start experiencing my days as a series of random incidents and accidents." ■ HENRI NOUWEN

6. "If you worry, why pray? If you pray, why worry?"

   ■ ANONYMOUS

   Phil 4:1&

7. "The only way you can fail at prayer is to not show up."

   ■ THOMAS KEATING

8. "Authentic prayer changes us—unmasks us—strips us— indicates where growth is needed. Authentic prayer never leads to complacency, but it needles us—makes us uneasy at times. It leads to true self-knowledge, to true humility."

   ■ ST. TERESA OF AVILA

9. "Don't put people down unless it's on your prayer list."

   ■ **STAN MICHALSKI**

10. "A real Christian prays with the Bible in one hand and the daily newspaper in the other." ■ **KARL BARTH**

Digital Connection

Suggested YouTube video: "Blessings" by Laura Story (with lyrics)

CHAPTER 16

The Beauty
of Friendship

"Friends are family you choose for yourself."

JANE ADDAMS

S piritual writer Alice Camille says that friendship should be named the eighth sacrament. She makes a good point. After all, the chief sign of a sacrament is that it bestows grace. For me personally, friendship has been one of the major sources of grace in my life. Where would I be today if I hadn't had childhood friends like G-G, Judy, Danny, and Ron? Or teenage friends like Kay, Mary Ann, Jimmy, and Fran? Or the many friends I had or have in my adult life? In this chapter we will look at some of the graces friendship bestows on us. Then we will reflect on Jesus' ability to befriend people. And finally, we will attempt to answer the question, "Can we be friends with God?"

The beauty of friendship lies in the many graces it can bestow on us. What graces? I have chosen four. First, friendship helps us grow in self-knowledge. By interacting with a good friend, we discover not only who our friend is but also who we are. As James Schall, SJ, writes, "The discovery of who we are is ultimately bound up with the discovery of another person."

Second, friendship boosts self-esteem. That happens when we realize, "This person actually likes *being with me*!" Which leads to the even more amazing realization, "This person actually *likes me*." Wow! How wonderful is that? And if the person is a good friend, they know our idiosyncrasies and shortcomings—and yet they still like us! Nothing gets better than that!

Third, friends broaden our perspective on life. Ordinarily we do not befriend a clone, that is, someone *exactly* like us. (We'll never find such a person anyway!) In a healthy friendship we will share some things in common, yes, but we will also have differences that can enrich us—if we allow them to. (Or differences that can also call us to ever greater patience!) My friends broaden my perspective by recommending books and movies for me, by dragging me into restaurants I might never had entered (recently an Ethiopian restaurant), and by giving me a new way of looking at an old problem.

A fourth grace friendship bestows on us is love. In fact, friendship is the school of love. Friendship teaches us how to receive and give love—concretely. Sooner or later friendship also teaches us two other essential components of love: how to say, "I'm sorry," and how to say, "I forgive you." In addition, friendship develops our ability to trust. And how important is trust in today's world? Popular writer and speaker Stephen Covey says this: "Trust is the glue of life. It's the most essential ingredient of effective communication. It's the foundational principle that holds all relationships."

What do Jesus' life and teachings reveal about friendship? One of the outstanding characteristics of Jesus' life was his ability to befriend people. On the eve of starting his public ministry, Jesus invited several individuals to walk and work with him. We usually focus on the twelve apostles, but Jesus had a larger "support group" of friends that included even Gentiles and women. In the gospels, Jesus is often shown dining with his friends and enjoying their company. Shortly before his death, he returned to Bethany to spend some quality time with his friends Lazarus, Mary, and Martha.

The Last Supper was a gathering of friends to celebrate the Passover meal. Ever since Da Vinci's fifteenth-century painting of the Last Supper, most depictions of this sacred meal show Jesus and the twelve apostles. But some scholars argue that others would have been present since it was the Passover meal. Those others would have included women—at least serving the meal—and their children. A contemporary painting of the Last Supper by Bohdan Piasecki includes six women and two children at the table. Regardless of who was at the Last Supper, it was during that meal that Jesus said to all present (and to us!), "You are my friends."

During his agony in Gethsemane, Jesus anxiously sought support from three very close friends, Peter, James, and John. They, like so many of his other friends, eventually deserted him during his trial and crucifixion. But Jesus never gave up on friendship. After his resurrection, he gave friendship another chance by forgiving those who had abandoned him.

Let us conclude this reflection with a few words about that question, "Can we be friends with God?" The Greek philosopher Aristotle claimed that true friendship requires three things: mutuality, reciprocity, and equality. Centuries later, St. Thomas Aquinas said that, with God, we do not have mutuality, reciprocity, or equality, but what we do have is Jesus. Aquinas maintained that Jesus is the bridge between God and us. Jesus makes friendship with God possible. The theologian Mindy G. Makant adds this point to the discussion. She notes that in Genesis, God speaks creation into existence: "Let there be light... let there be plants... let there be animals." So too, at the Last Supper, when Jesus calls us friends, his "words that we are friends make it so." In other words, Jesus speaks friendship with God into existence.

But how do we nurture friendship with God, friendship with Jesus? St. John Chrysostom offers this suggestion: we nurture our friendship with God by befriending those who are already friends with God. He cites two such groups: the saints and the poor. Chrysostom says we should pray to befriend the saints, and we should practice hospitality and generosity in order to befriend the poor. Two ways, therefore, to pursue our friendship with God are prayer and generosity.

It seems appropriate to end this reflection with a quote on friendship by one of the saints who generously gave his life for a stranger. St. Maximilian Kolbe, a Franciscan friar, was imprisoned in Auschwitz during the Nazi Regime. Kolbe offered to die in the place of another prisoner. His offer was accepted. As a result, Kolbe endured a slow, agonizing death by starvation and, eventually, a lethal injection. These are the words about friendship from this holy and selfless man: "God sends us friends to be our firm support in the whirlpool of struggle. In the company of friends, we will find strength to obtain our sublime ideal."

Questions for Reflection

1. This chapter gives four graces friendship can bestow: self-knowledge, self-esteem, a broadening of our perspective, and love. Have you experienced these through the friendships you have? If so, how?

2. Are there any other graces you have received from your friends?

3. Can you say, "God is my friend" or "Jesus is my friend"? If so, what helps you to say that? If not, what prevents you from saying that?

I Call You Friend

I call you friend. For you are home to me.
Within the shelter of your good company,
I safely lay my burdens down.

I call you friend. For you are healing for me.
You listen to all I have to say and, in so doing,
I am made more whole.

I call you friend. For you are a priceless gift for me,
one I did not earn. But one I receive anew each day
with wonder, joy, and gratitude.

I call you friend. For without you I would not be me.
With you, I am more of who I want to be.

I call you friend. In part, we are alike,
sharing deep values we seldom have to articulate.
In part, we are different. Our differences mark our uniqueness,
broaden our perspective, spur our growth, and,
at times, hone our patience.

I call you friend. For you encourage me
not merely by your words, but by the example of your
own strivings, questionings, and yearnings.
You are my cheerleader, rousing me to stay in the game of life.
You are my ground control, confirming where
I am and where I am heading.

God enters our lives in countless creative ways.
One way for me, my friend, is you.

Digital Connection

Suggested YouTube video: "Thank You"
by No Limitz (with lyrics)

CHAPTER 17

Say It with Beauty

*"The best thing to do with the best things
in life is to give them away."*

DOROTHY DAY

I was filled with grief when my brother John passed away. He was only sixty-five and we were very close. On that early morning in October when he died, I was blessed to be with him. When I returned home, I posted the announcement of his death on our Sisters of Notre Dame community email, asking for prayers for him and his family. Later that day, the doorbell rang. When I opened the door, there stood a dear friend of mine, a Sister of Notre Dame. Because she lived almost twenty miles away, I was surprised to see her. But there she was, holding in her hands a small potted primrose, bright yellow. She handed me the flower, hugged me warmly, and said softly, "I'm so sorry, Melannie." We exchanged a few words and cried a little, and then she left. I was deeply moved by her expression of sympathy—both her presence and the flower. Sometimes a simple gift of beauty says more than many words could ever convey.

"Say it with flowers" is the slogan created in 1917 by the Federal

Telegraph Delivery. The slogan reflects what people have been doing for centuries: giving beautiful flowers to convey messages of love, happiness, and sorrow. So popular was this custom that, over the years, specific flowers became associated with specific messages. Red roses convey eternal love; yellow roses, friendship; sunflowers, happiness; geraniums, an apology.

Flowers are a beautiful way to express our love and appreciation for someone. But there are other ways too. Since most of us already have enough "stuff," instead of buying your loved ones another *thing*, why not give the gift of a shared experience of beauty? Here is an example. My sister's favorite musical was *The Music Man*. One year she was visiting her oldest son and his family in upper state New York. For her birthday (which was coming up), he surprised her with two tickets to a local theater production of *The Music Man*. Before the show, he took her out to dinner—just the two of them. Then they went to the play. Afterward, my sister told me it was one of the best birthday presents she had ever received. Why? First, she got to enjoy a fine dinner and her favorite musical. Then, more important, she had time to enjoy her son, an experience she cherished.

We can express our love with all kinds of shared experiences. I still remember a birthday gift I received many years ago from several friends. Knowing my love for animals, they took me to the zoo for the day. Other such gifts include visiting the botanical gardens, enjoying a concert, attending a sporting event, playing a round of golf (even miniature golf), having a picnic, or just sitting on the back porch in the evening with a glass of wine.

There are smaller and ordinary ways to give to others too. St. Teresa of Calcutta always stressed the importance of a smile, a listening ear, a helping hand. She was fond of saying, "It's not how much you give, but how much love you put into giving." Sometimes

91

we give by allowing others to give to us. In the words of poet Maya Angelou, "When we give cheerfully and accept gratefully, everyone is blessed."

Sometimes people invent ingenious ways to express their love. Here's a unique gift I received from my brother John many years ago. The date was April 11, 1971. I was living in a boarding school on our provincial center property at the time. It was Easter Sunday—and my brother John's thirtieth birthday. John lived nearby with his wife and five-year-old son. In his spare time, John liked to fly. He and a few friends had pooled their money and bought an open cockpit biplane, a 1941 blue and yellow Stearman.

John would fly over our provincial center regularly. I could always tell his plane, because it made a distinctive *putt-putt-putt* sound. When I heard it, I would run outside and wave to him. When he spotted me, he would tip his wings. It was beautiful! On this particular Easter, I called John to wish him a happy birthday. He asked, "Are you going to be home this afternoon?" "Yes," I said. He replied, "Good. I'm flying over today. It's Easter, and I hear there are bunnies everywhere!"

Later that afternoon, when I heard his plane, I ran outside. He was flying fairly low, so I could see him sitting in the rear cockpit. He raised his arm to wave, and a moment later I saw a tiny parachute fluttering to the ground. Surprised and excited, I ran to the nearby field where it had landed. It was a small, stuffed bunny—a blue one—hitched to a parachute made from a kitchen towel. I picked it up and waved it in the air so John could see that I had retrieved it. John tipped his wings and flew slowly away. That day John, using his skill as a pilot and his love for me, gave me a gift of beauty I will never forget.

I think God also uses beauty to say things to us all the time. God says, "I love you," by giving us flowers of every conceivable color, size, shape, texture, and scent. With every sunrise, God says, "Here's the gift of another day for you." With every sunset, God says, "Here's another night for you to sleep and regain your strength." And God adds, "Don't worry. I'm keeping vigil while you sleep."

God says, "Look what I made for you," by giving us the wide variety of animals to share this earthly life with us. Earth would be a lonely world without these animals—especially our pets. And imagine how empty the world would be without birds chirping in our trees, soaring in the air, or dining at our birdfeeders. God also says, "I am with you always," by giving us a beating heart and the strength we need to face hard times.

But God speaks to us most clearly by giving us Jesus. At Jesus' transfiguration, a voice from the cloud says, "This is my beloved Son. Listen to him" (Mk 9:7). The fact that you are reading a book such as this is a good indication that you are someone who is listening to Jesus and following his Way.

Questions for Reflection

1. What are some of the gifts of beauty you have you received from others?

2. What gifts of beauty have you given to others?

3. Have you ever given or received a gift of a beautiful shared experience? If so, what was that experience like for you? If not, might you consider giving such a gift?

Say It with Beauty

"Say it with flowers," the flower people tell us.
But I believe any gift of beauty will do.
Yes, say it with flowers, potted or cut,
from the shop in town or your own backyard.
Say it with a meal, lovingly prepared, artistically presented.
Say it with two reserved seats for the play,
the game, the concert, the movie,
the six-hour river cruise that nourishes your souls.
Say it with a personal note, handwritten.
Say it with a book, a night of dancing,
a day at the zoo, the art museum, the observatory.
Say it with a framed photograph,
a hand-crafted afghan,
an offer to help, accompany, take care of it.
Say it with chocolate chip cookies,
kolacky, or a cake decorated by a six-year-old.
Yes, say it with beauty. Say it with love.
And be assured: whatever beauty-filled way you choose to say it,
you will say it well. Very well.

Digital Connection

Suggested YouTube video: "Simple Gifts" by Yo-Yo Ma and
Alison Krause (video by Vickie Burns)

CHAPTER 18

Beauty and Brokenness

*"There is no perfection, only beautiful
versions of brokenness."*

SHANNON ALDER

 priest recently posed this question to his congregation: "What if you received a text message from Jesus saying, 'I'm on my way. I'll be at your house by 8:00 this evening.' What would you do?"

Most of us would spring into action. We would begin to get our house ready to receive such an honored guest. We would clear the dirty dishes in the sink and straighten up the living room. We might even throw the stuff that was lying around—old magazines and clothes—into a closet. The last thing we would want Jesus to see was that mess in our closet.

But, said the priest, "Jesus is not coming to see our clean house and orderly lives. Jesus is coming for the mess." Wasn't that how Jesus himself described his mission? He said he was a doctor coming to care for the ill, not the perfectly healthy. To the disciples of John the Baptist, he said he had come to make the blind see, the lame walk, the lepers clean. In other words, Jesus came to serve imperfect people—like me, like you. He came to see what we have shoved into our closet. And sometimes what is hiding in there is our brokenness.

Brokenness can take many forms. It can be our sins and failings such as our selfishness, pettiness, impatience, dishonesty, greed, prejudice. Our brokenness can include other painful aspects of our life such as anxiety, fear, anger, loneliness, and grief. In short, our brokenness is anywhere we hurt. When Jesus comes to us, we need to say to him as we would a doctor, "Here is where it hurts, Jesus," or, "Here is where *I* hurt, Jesus." By doing so, we are exposing our brokenness to Jesus' healing love.

On one level, our brokenness is painful. But on another level, it can be beautiful too. This analogy might help. Many centuries ago, Japanese bowl makers had a venerable tradition. If a bowl cracked, they would not toss the bowl aside. Rather, they would mend the bowl by filling the crack with liquid gold. Instead of concealing the crack, the gold, when hardened, called attention to it. The artists believed that the cracks made the bowl more beautiful and more valuable. (You can see some of these bowls in the video and song suggested at the end of this chapter.)

In our spiritual lives, we have experiences that damage us, that cause cracks in us: failure, betrayal, addiction, shame, loss. Every significant trauma can be a shattering: abuse, serious injury, debilitating illness. Where is there beauty in such brokenness?

I believe one way brokenness can be beautiful is this: it can expose our human limitations, the vagaries of living, and the unmet desires of our heart. Our human failings remind us of our need for others and for God. And that is good and beautiful! The vagaries and uncertainties of life can help us to put our trust in the one constant we do have in life: our loving God who is always with us. How beautiful! And our unmet desires attest that nothing on earth can satisfy the deepest longings of our heart. Only God can do that. Again, how beautiful it is to know that!

Another way there is beauty in brokenness is this: it can lead us to God, to Jesus. Many saints came to God precisely through their brokenness. St. Julie Billiart, foundress of the Sisters of Notre Dame, did not have a perfect life. As a young girl in pre-revolutionary France, she witnessed an assassination attempt on her father. Though he was unharmed, Julie was psychologically wounded by the trauma—so much so, she was unable to walk or speak clearly, a condition she endured for decades. But during this period of pain and immobility, she gathered children around her bed and taught them about the goodness of God. Her infirmity nurtured her own intimacy with God and her deep desire to educate others—especially "the daughters of the poor." In time, Julie was cured of her paralysis. Today there are three congregations that trace their lineage back to her, serving people all over the world. Talk about beauty rising from brokenness!

Our brokenness, imperfections, and even sin, once acknowledged, can underscore our need for God's love and mercy. In addition, they can also instill within us qualities much needed in today's world, namely, love and compassion. Our brokenness can bring us together as families, local communities, nations, and even the world. Most of us remember exactly where we were on September 11, 2001, when the twin towers came crashing down. It was a horrific event in American history. Yet many of us also remember feeling more united with one another—especially with those who had lost loved ones that day. In the days that followed, we as a nation seemed to be kinder to our loved ones as well as to total strangers. Years ago, the writer Henry Nouwen wrote a book called *The Wounded Healer*. In it he maintained that it is primarily out of our own woundedness that we minister effectively to the wounds of others. The experience of our own brokenness helps us serve others with greater understanding and tenderness.

When I think of brokenness, two images come to my mind. The first image is one Jesus himself gave us: the grain of wheat being buried in the ground. That image will be the focus of the meditation that concludes this chapter.

The second image of brokenness is, of course, Jesus on the cross. Many representations of Jesus' crucifixion are "sanitized." But a few years back, one artist fashioned a crucifix that was very realistic. At the first showing of the artwork, one woman said to him, "Sir, I do not like your crucifix. It is too awful." He replied, "Madam, it was an awful event." Jesus' brokenness on the cross was awful. But the love he displayed on the cross is "awe-full" too, that is, filled with awe and wonder.

Barbara Brown Taylor, an Episcopal priest, says, "We need a God who knows about pain....What the cross teaches us is not God's power...to end human pain. It is, instead, the power to pick up the shattered pieces and make something holy out of them." And, we might add, to make something beautiful from our brokenness.

Questions for Reflection

1. Take time to reflect on some of the brokenness you have experienced in life. Have any of these experiences helped make you a better person? If so, how?

2. How are you ministering to the wounded—even in small ways—in your family, neighborhood, parish, local community, and beyond?

3. Take time to gaze at a crucifix. Does it move you in any way? If so, how? If you could say anything to Jesus on the cross, what would you say?

And the Stalk Said...

How does a grain of wheat feel as it is planted in the soil? To answer that, I imagine interviewing a stalk of wheat, for every stalk was once a grain. Here is what the stalk might say:

"I liked being a grain of wheat. I was proud of who I was: Golden. Smooth. Perfectly intact. But then some farmer dug a hole and tossed me into it. 'What's going on?' I asked. But my question was met with silence. Then the dirt came pouring down on me. I protested, 'Hey! You're burying me alive! Stop!' But no one heard me.

"I sat in total darkness. Afraid. Then I felt something. Moisture. At first I thought, 'Good. I won't die of thirst.' But then I began to get soggy. I sensed my golden color was fading. My smooth exterior became wrinkly. My intactness was breached as I was split asunder. I whimpered, 'I'm dying. This is the end of me.'

"Then something amazing happened. Out of my shriveled, broken, dying self, two shoots emerged. One began pushing upward, the other downward—both powered by a force within and beyond me. As my root went down, my shoot went up until it broke through the soil and into the brightness of the sun. I was no longer a grain of wheat— but something better: a *stalk* of wheat. From me would come forth many, many grains of wheat that would help feed the people of the world."

In closing, the stalk said: "Trust the Farmer. Befriend silence and darkness. Embrace transformation. Willingly relinquish your intactness. Believe. For the Ending is really the Beginning."

Digital Connection

Suggested YouTube video: "Japanese Bowl" by Peter Mayer

CHAPTER 19

The Beauty of Service

*"Life's most persistent and urgent question is,
what are you doing for others?"*

MARTIN LUTHER KING, JR.

I t was a Monday morning. I decided to go to a nearby parish for the 7:30 Mass. As I sat in the small eucharistic chapel, I noticed the pastor come into the large gathering space of the church. He was fully vested for Mass. As the people came into the church, he greeted them.

Then suddenly he left. I thought he had forgotten something in the sacristy. But a minute later he emerged pushing a vacuum cleaner. He plugged it in, turned it on, and proceeded to vacuum a small area of the gathering space. When he finished, he wrapped the cord around the sweeper, and pushed it back to where he had gotten it.

This little vignette made me smile. First, this priest noticed there was something on the carpet. Second, he didn't wait until the cleaning crew arrived. He took care of it himself. (Personally, I was a little surprised he even knew where the sweeper was kept!) And third, he did the little chore cheerfully, not grudgingly.

The image of that priest, fully vested for Mass, pushing a vacuum cleaner edified me. It showed just how dedicated he was to serving his parish community—in all kinds of ways. Yes, he served his parish when presiding at Mass, hearing confessions, attending parish council meetings, providing counsel, visiting the sick, and anointing the dying. But his service extended beyond these "official duties." By doing this simple task of vacuuming, he was beautifying the church. And beyond that, his action demonstrated that we bring more beauty into the world precisely through our selfless service.

In his book *Beauty: The Invisible Embrace*, John O'Donohue writes, "Everywhere there is tenderness, care, and kindness, there is beauty." Similarly, we can say everywhere there is selfless service, there is beauty. Jesus underscored the importance of service through both his teachings and his example. On the night before he died, as he dined with his friends, Jesus got up, took a towel, and tied it around his waist. In other words, he made a makeshift apron. Then he bent down and proceeded to wash the feet of his disciples, a task ordinarily assigned to a servant or slave. As someone has so aptly said, "Jesus donned an apron and redefined success." For Jesus, success was not power, material wealth, or worldly achievement. Success was service. It was about wearing aprons.

Sometimes we wear actual aprons. When I was growing up, my mother wore an apron every day. She donned it early in the morning and didn't take it off until the dishes were done after supper. She did everything in that apron: stoked the coal furnace, cooked our meals, washed clothes, cleaned the house, picked green beans, and even fed the chickens. No wonder when my mother passed away, my sister and I both wanted one of her aprons. Her aprons were a symbol of who she was. Today when I put on my mother's apron, I kiss it reverently—just as a priest vesting for Mass kisses the stole he drapes around his neck. To me, my mother's apron is holy. It was what she wore all those years as she joyfully served her way into eternity.

There are other symbols of service besides vacuum cleaners and aprons. Take firetrucks. I have always been fascinated by firetrucks. They are so big and flashy, so loud and fast. In addition, they are stuffed with fascinating equipment: ladders, hoses, axes, fire extinguishers, ventilating equipment, and even onboard water reservoirs. But what intrigues me the most about firetrucks are the firefighters themselves. These men and women serve people—often strangers. When a call comes in, they drop everything and race to the emergency—whether it is a house fire, a car accident, an explosion, a skyscraper ablaze, or a forest in flames. Once there, they go about their work with energy and skill. They never ask the people they are serving, "What will you give me if I help you?" They never ask, "What religion do you profess?" Or, "Whom did you vote for in the last election?" No, they just serve, no questions asked. That's unselfish service at its best.

Some professions are obviously service oriented—or they should be: doctors and nurses, law enforcement personnel, educators, clergy, and such. But almost every kind of work is a form of service for others. Take parenting. Is there any other "work" more service oriented than that? Other forms of service are done by store clerks, waitpersons, bus drivers, airline personnel, cooks, snowplow drivers, sanitation workers, receptionists, and even people collecting tolls on highways.

One special kind of service is volunteerism. About 25 to 30 percent of Americans volunteer in some capacity. Many of these serve religious organizations, educational or youth programs, and social establishments. Volunteers can be found reading at Mass, coaching youth teams, distributing food at a soup kitchen, serving on boards, cleaning up neighborhoods, building houses for the homeless, pushing wheelchairs in hospitals, babysitting grandkids, working at polling stations, fundraising for museums, counting baby birds in the park, and much more. Without volunteers, local communities would face devastating gaps in much needed services.

The good news is that volunteerism not only improves the lives of others but also improves the lives of the volunteers by keeping them active, connected with others, and a part of something bigger than themselves. But it is not enough to simply serve another. *How* we serve is crucial. St. Francis of Assisi said it well: "It is not fitting, when one is in God's service, to have a gloomy face." Mahatma Gandhi echoes those words: "Service, which is rendered without joy, helps neither the servant nor the served. But all other pleasures and possessions pale into nothingness before service which is rendered in a spirit of joy."

Questions for Reflection

1. When you think of the word *service*, what images or individuals come to your mind? Why?

2. Think of a time when you were on the receiving end of someone's joyful service. Recall some of the details of that experience. How did the experience make you feel?

3. Be mindful of the volunteers you encounter this week. You might want to thank them for their service.

Your Gaze and Touch and Word

Jesus, your gaze and touch and word
empowered people to love and service.

At your gaze,
the fishermen left their nets on the shore,
and Matthew walked away from his customs post,
all to follow you.
At your glance,
Peter was moved to profound sorrow
for his threefold denial of you.

At your touch,
Peter's mother-in-law got up and began to serve;
the dead son of the widow of Nain sat up and began to speak;
the woman, bent over like a candy cane,
stood up straight and tall
and began to sing her praises of thanksgiving to God.

At your word,
Lazarus stumbled forth from the darkness of the tomb,
and Zacchaeus climbed down from the sycamore tree
and changed his whole way of living.
And Mary Magdalene, recognizing your voice in the garden,
ran back to the disciples with the good news of your resurrection.

Jesus, gaze upon me. Touch me. Speak my name.
So I too may be empowered to follow you
in joyful love and service. Amen.

Digital Connection

Suggested YouTube video: "The Servant Song"
(meansusa—sung by Bukas Palad Ministries)

CHAPTER 20

Beauty and Grief

*"How lucky am I to have something that
makes saying goodbye so hard."*

WINNIE THE POOH

I am no authority on grief. But over the years I have experienced grief, and I have shared in the grief of others. Based on that, I have put down a few thoughts on grief—and beauty.

What is grief? Grief is the emotional suffering that accompanies loss. When we think of grief, we usually think of the pain experienced when a loved one dies. But we grieve other losses too: the loss of a job, a pet, our youth, our health, a home, our independence. We are often sensitive when someone is grieving the loss of a loved one, but can we be sensitive when someone is grieving the loss of their cat, their hearing, their accustomed way of doing things?

We do not necessarily grieve in the same way. Some people cannot stop crying. Others shed few tears. Some want to be alone. Others do not want to be alone. Some become listless. Others, hyper. Still others, angry. Some want to talk about their grief. Others want to grieve in silence. We must learn to recognize and respect the way others grieve—and the way we ourselves grieve.

Grief can come in unpredictable waves. In the initial throes of grief, we might think, "I will never get over this loss." But time does have a way of lessening the pain. At least for a while. But weeks, months, or even years later, we can be hit by an unexpected wave of grief. Our loved one's anniversary of death, their birthday, their favorite song, a particular place we frequented—all can have the power to overwhelm us with pain and even tears. The best book I have read on grief is C.S. Lewis' book, *A Grief Observed*, a journal he kept after his wife's death. In poignant entries, he describes the various stages of his grief. At one point, for example, he writes, "Her absence is like the sky, spread over everything."

Grieving is the way we relearn the world. When we suffer a significant loss, our world is radically changed. And *we* are radically changed. If our spouse dies, we lose one identity (wife or husband) and take on a new one (widow or widower). When our last parent dies, we may feel orphaned. When a sibling dies, we have lost a "fellow nestling," that is, someone who shared the same childhood nest with us. When my sister Mary Ann died a few years ago, I was overcome with grief. I had lost not only my only sister: I had lost my best friend. I also lost her unique love for me expressed in countless tender words and thoughtful ways. I lost part of my history too—all those shared experiences growing up together that no one else knew in quite the same way. With her death, I had to learn to live without her visible companionship and support. And I had to learn a new way of expressing my love to her, because the former ways were gone.

As painful as grief can be, it still possesses a beauty all its own. I like to say that grief is the underside of love. When a loved one dies, we grieve because we have loved and have been loved. It is as simple as that. There is no clearer proof of the beauty and power of human love than the pain we experience when the object of our love has been taken away from us. Grief also underscores the essential goodness and meaningfulness of life. If people were not good and things did not matter, we would never grieve their loss. But grief says: people are good, things do matter, love is an amazing gift, and life has meaning. That is grief's essential beauty.

We Christians have an additional help when grieving. We believe that the separation from our loved ones through death is only temporary, not permanent. As Demetrius Dumm, OSB, reminds us: "The goodbyes we say to our loved ones at death are not final. 'Hello' has the last word!" We believe Jesus has conquered death through the power of his resurrection. The pain of our grief challenges us: "Do you really believe this 'stuff' about Jesus' death and resurrection and life everlasting? Do you really believe you will be reunited with your loved ones after death?" Hopefully, in time, our grief will lead us to Jesus. The father of the boy having convulsions begged Jesus, "Have compassion on us and help us." Jesus said, "Everything is possible to one who has faith." The man cried out, "I do believe, help my unbelief!" (Mk 9:22–25). His words remind us, our faith does not have to be perfect for Jesus to respond to our needs.

Jesuit priest Gerry Stockhausen gave a brief homily on these words of Jesus: "The kingdom of heaven is like a treasure buried in a field, which a person finds and hides again, and out of joy goes and sells all that he has and buys that field." The priest said, "If you want the treasure, you have to take the whole field, everything in it. What you treasure and what you wish wasn't part of the deal. It's like marriage vows: for better, for worse... good days, bad days." Grief is a part of the field called life. At first, we might think grief is not part of the "treasure"; it is part of the "worse." But when we realize grief reveals the beauty of things, of places, of experiences, and (most of all) of people, then grief itself becomes part of the hidden treasure in the field of life.

The concluding reflection in this chapter is about the death of my sister. A little background. Mary Ann was seventy-seven, a widow, mother of five, and grandmother of nine. The day before Thanksgiving she learned she was filled with cancer: stomach, kidneys, liver. Prior to the diagnosis, she was essentially asymptomatic. After weighing her options, she decided to forego dialysis, radiation, and chemo, saying, "It's all in God's hands." And later, "I'm ready to die." She was transported to hospice where she died ten days later surrounded by us, her family. I am sharing these journal excerpts below because they express my thoughts and feelings *while I was grieving*. Perhaps you may find them helpful for your own times of loss.

Questions for Reflection

1. What have been some of the losses you have had to face in life? Did you grieve these losses? If so, how?

2. What has helped you to deal with your own grief?

3. Have you ever helped someone else to deal with his or her grief? If so, what did you do to help?

Mourning Mary Ann

+ The sympathy cards keep pouring in. And I appreciate each one—honest I do. But today I say, "Enough already!" Each card underscores the depth of my loss.

+ People ask, "How are you, Melannie?" How do I answer that? Do I say, "Fine"? No. My sister is gone. How could I be fine? From now on, my "fine" will always be tempered by the loss of Mary Ann.

+ I wish I had had more time to talk to her those last few days. And I wish she had had more strength to stay awake and speak to us, to me. But there I go again, trying to orchestrate the perfect death...instead of giving thanks for all the time we did have with her as she lay dying. And all those countless times over the years that I did have to talk with her—whether on the phone, across the table at a restaurant, beside her on the couch, with her in the park, next to her in the car. I tell myself, "Regret less. Give thanks more."

+ I feel strangely immune from pain. With Mary Ann's death I've been dealt one of the hardest blows life can give. And yet, here I am still alive. Limping from the blow, yes. But still walking.

+ It's her fault my grief is so great. If only she hadn't loved me so much. If only we hadn't gotten along so well. If only we hadn't enjoyed each other's company so much. If only I hadn't loved her so much. If only... If only...

+ When I crawled into bed last night, the tears came. Finally. I haven't cried since the funeral. But last night, alone in the dark, I cried on and off until after midnight. I whimpered more than sobbed. My mind was flooded with questions. How could she be filled with cancer and nobody know it? Not her. Not her doctor. There's anger in my question. If only she had known sooner, maybe she could have received treatment. Maybe she could have had more time with us. But then I hear her words, "It's all in God's hands." She *really* believed that. Can I?

+ She told us she was ready to die. But how did she "get ready"? She got ready by embracing the blessings and challenges life set before her: being faithful to John, raising five kids, working at the deli, welcoming in-laws and grandchildren into the circle of her love, doing small acts of kindness for her neighbors, praying every day, feeding the birds, volunteering at the animal shelter, appreciating the beauties of nature. She got ready by dealing with ambiguity, sorrow, disappointment, loneliness, worry, and fear with her gentle yet steady faith. She got ready to die the way we all get ready to die, by the way we live our lives.

+ I had forgotten how tired grieving makes you.

+ I will miss being known so well.

+ I feel as if I am walking around in an envelope of grief. Part of me wants to break out. Part of me wants to stay inside.

Digital Connection

Suggested YouTube video: "Just Be Held" (with lyrics) by Casting Crowns (Video by Yanina R)

CHAPTER 21

The Beauty of Humor

"Laughter is carbonated holiness."

ANNE LAMOTT

A few years back I was given a sabbatical. I went on an Alaskan cruise with another Sister of Notre Dame. It was the trip of a lifetime! For a week we sailed the inner coastal waterway, surrounded by deep blue water, snow-capped mountains, lush greenery, and wildlife galore. While sailing, I sent a few postcards home to the two sisters I lived with. In one of them I said, "When we return to our cabin in the evening, our beds are turned down and there's a piece of chocolate on our pillows!"

When I got home and went up to my bedroom, sure enough, my bed was turned down. And on my pillow was a single M&M! A plain one! Not even a peanut one! Next to it was this sign: "That for one more night you may be treated in the manner to which you are now accustomed. But know that tomorrow everything deteriorates to normal!" It was signed, "Your loving Sisters at St. Mary's Convent."

How lucky we are if we live and work with people who have a good sense of humor. For humor is an integral part of the beauty of life. Sometimes I think we could use an Eleventh Commandment: "Thou shalt smile and laugh regularly." For humor is filled with blessings.

First, humor helps us to keep things in perspective. I once taught at a high school where the principal hung a poster on the inside of her office door. When she sat at her desk during a conference with a student, or parents, or a teacher, she saw that poster. They did not. It was a picture of the Milky Way with its 100 million stars swirling around. There was an arrow pointing to a teeny, weeny dot—our sun—on the outer fringes of the galaxy. Next to the arrow were these words: YOU ARE HERE. That visual helped that principal to keep things in perspective.

Humor relieves stress. When we are anxious or worried about something, sometimes a little child will say something funny that dispels our anxiety—like this:

Four-year-old: Can we get a kitten?
Mother: No, I'm allergic. We can't be in the same house.
Four-year-old: You could sleep outside.

Father: Someday you'll have feelings for boys.
Six-year-old daughter: I already have feelings for boys.
Father: Really?
Six-year-old daughter: Yes, they make me mad.

A four-year-old girl was taken to Mass for the first time by her grandparents. When the priest and deacon processed up the aisle, the girl turned to her grandfather and whispered, "Which one is God?"

Said a five-year-old: Grandma is so good with kids, why doesn't she have any of her own?

Humor can keep us humble. It reminds us that we are not in charge of life. And it often points out our basic human limitations. Here are two stories that illustrate this:

A young man was sitting at a bar drinking a bottle of beer. Two young women at one of the tables caught his eye. One of them smiled at him. He smiled back. She smiled at him again. After a few moments, he picked up his beer and sauntered over to the table to meet her. Imagine his surprise when he got to the table and realized he was holding the ketchup bottle!

Fred believed the number five was his lucky number. He was born on May 5, 1955. He had five kids and lived at 555 East 55th Street. On his 55th birthday, he saw there was a horse running in the fifth race named Numero Cinco. So he ran to the bank and took out $500. Five minutes before the race, he went to the fifth window and put the money on that horse. Sure enough, his horse came in fifth!

The saints knew the importance of humor. For three years St. Catherine of Siena was tormented by doubts, demonic visions, and taunting voices. She said she finally "banished them with laughter." Immediately Jesus appeared to her. St. Teresa of Avila penned these famous words, "From silly devotions and sour-faced saints, Good Lord, deliver us!" This wisdom is attributed to St. Ignatius: "Laugh and grow strong." And when St. John Bosco was dying, he was asked what his two favorite books were. He said, "The New Testament and my joke book."

The British writer William Barclay said, "A gloomy Christian is a contradiction in terms." That does not mean we have to be smiling and laughing all the time, of course. After all, life is filled with difficulties. There is much sadness in the world. We sometimes experience great heartache. But our Christian faith places all of these painful realities against the backdrop of God's unfailing love for us. In his letter, "Principles of Catholic Theology," Pope Benedict XVI wrote: "By its very essence, by its very nature, Christian belief is 'glad tidings.'"

Here are a few more jokes:

The convent van was getting old so the Mother Superior called a car dealer and asked what a new van would cost. He said gently, "Are you sitting down, Sister?" She replied, "I'm kneeling, Mr. Smith."

Two women were looking at greeting cards. The one said to the other, "I'm looking for a card that says, 'Your love is priceless' for under $5."

If you cross a bee and a lightning bug, you get a bee that can work at night.

A committee is a group of people who talk for hours to produce a result known as "minutes."

Did you know you have the right to remain silent even when you're not being arrested?

Is ignorance or apathy destroying this country? Answer: I don't know and I don't care!

And finally, here are three comments by kindergartners to their teachers:

You're pretty for an old person.

You aren't as mean as some kids say you are—just loud.

I named my bunny after you.

Years ago there was a TV show called *Candid Camera*, on which people were secretly filmed doing amusing things. At the end of each segment, a voice would say: "Smile! You're on *Candid Camera*." Our sense of humor says something similar to us: "Smile! You're on a beautiful and remarkable journey—and God is with you every step of the way!"

Questions for Reflection

1. What role does humor play in your life?

2. Recall a few humorous things that happened to you recently.

3. What helps you to keep your sense of humor alive?

Quotations on Humor...
Do you like any of these?

1. "Humor is a prelude to faith, and laughter is the beginning of prayer." ■ **REINHOLD NIEBUHR**

2. "A smile is a curve that sets everything straight."
   ■ **PHYLLIS DILLER**

3. "Laughing is and will always be the best form of therapy."
   ■ **DAU VOIRE**

4. "Laughter is an instant vacation." ■ **MILTON BERLE**

5. "When humor goes, there goes civilization."
   ■ **ERMA BOMBECK**

6. "He deserves paradise who makes his companions laugh."
   ■ **QURAN**

7. "Laughter has no foreign accent." ■ **PAUL LOWNEY**

8. "Laughter is the foundation of reconciliation."
   ■ **ST. FRANCES DE SALES**

9. "Trouble knocked at the door but, hearing laughter, hurried away." ■ **BEN FRANKLIN**

10. "The one who laughs lasts!"
    ■ **MARY PETTIBONE POOLE**

11. "Laughter is the shortest distance between two people."
    ■ **VICTOR BORGE**

12. "When you laugh, you get a glimpse of God."
    ■ **MERRILY BELGUM**

Digital Connection

Suggested YouTube video: "How Can I Keep from Singing"
by Audrey Assad or Chris Tomlin

CHAPTER 22

Creating Beauty of Our Own

"May we be carriers and multipliers of love."

MARGARET SILF

A book on beauty would not be complete without mentioning the importance of creating beauty of our own. As we already said, God is *the* Creator of beauty. If we are made in the image and likeness of God, then we too are to be creators of beauty. We could say that the impulse to create beauty is embedded in our human DNA.

When we look around our world, we see a world in desperate need of beauty. There is already enough ugliness—especially the ugliness of hatred, war, poverty, greed, violence, and other injustices of all kinds. This ugliness spawns division, fear, loneliness, and a sense of hopelessness. In the sixteenth century, St. John of the Cross wrote these famous words, "Where there is no love, put love and you will find love." For our purposes, we can say, "Where there is no *beauty*, put *beauty* and you will find *beauty*."

Once again, I quote Demetrius Dumm, OSB. He wrote years ago

that we are not meant merely "to notice and feast on beauty." We are "to create beauty where it does not exist." How do we do this? Some of us might possess the desire and the talent to create beauty in word, gesture, story, drawing, symbol, color, song, or dance. We do not have to be a Michelangelo, an Emily Dickinson, an Ella Fitzgerald, or a Gene Kelly to create such beauty. We can be Joe Hartman with a small chunk of wood and a pocketknife, or Sandy Sabbetto with a journal and a pen, or Tim Adams singing in a church choir, or Mary Benish dancing with her grandchildren in the backyard.

There are other ways, besides creating a work of art, to bring beauty into the world. St. Teresa of Calcutta said, "Every time you smile at someone, it is an action of love, a gift to that person, a beautiful thing." So, something as simple as a smile can bring more beauty into a world where individuals are starving for attention, desperate for recognition, or longing to connect with another human being in a meaningful way. Sometimes bridging the gap between you and me, between us and them, starts with a smile, a wave, or a nod.

Thich Nhat Hanh, a Vietnamese Buddhist monk, offers another way we can bring beauty into our world. He wrote, "To be beautiful means to be yourself." This suggests that the more we are becoming that unique person God is calling us to be, the more beautiful we are. I once saw this idea expressed on a poster that said, "Be-YOU-tiful."

But by far, the best way we bring beauty into the world is by doing loving things. Some people do this in dramatic ways. Sister Rosemary Dowd, RSCJ, ministers in a prison. She was led to this ministry after reflecting on that quote by St. John of the Cross I used earlier. Her reflecting led her to raise this question: Where else is love lacking so much as in a prison? She felt that God was saying to her, "This is where I want you to serve." She met with her community leader and said, "I'll do whatever you want me to, but I think God is asking me to go to jail!" After more prayer and dialogue, her community gave her the green light. That was forty years ago! Sister Rosemary has served in prison ever since, bringing beauty there—and finding beauty there too.

One individual who brought beauty into the world in a dramatic way was Joseph P. Riley, former mayor of Charleston, South Carolina. Riley was thirty-two when he was elected mayor in 1975. He became one of the longest-serving mayors in US history, serving ten terms before his retirement in 2016. During his forty years as mayor, Riley led a movement that made Charleston a more beautiful city. He began by leading the protest to have the Confederate flag removed from above the statehouse. Then he worked with others to redevelop the central business district, making it more pedestrian friendly and architecturally pleasing to the eye. He brought the arts back to the city, making sure that some of the concerts and art festivals were free so anyone could attend. Under his leadership the beautiful Waterfront Park was constructed, allowing all people free access to the riverside. He considers his "most important work" the International African American Museum being built on the former wharf where over 40 percent of the slaves brought to this country "took their first steps." Riley is an advocate for beauty, saying that when you insist on beauty in public places, "it's a gift to every citizen in every walk of life."

But we do not have to be a mayor of a large city to bring beauty into the world. Sometimes you can be a student in a small Catholic elementary school in a semi-rural area. The children at St. Helen School in Newbury, Ohio, bring beauty into the world in a small but unique way. These children make "breakfast bags" that are given to people at food distribution centers after they have received their allotment of food. The children start with plain white bags. But before they fill them with food they have brought, they decorate the bags in beautiful ways. They draw flowers, trees, birds, hearts, crosses, peace symbols. Often, they use pretty stickers and write short messages on the bags, such as "God bless you" or "God loves you." Other times they write inspirational quotes. Then they form an assembly line and fill the breakfast bags with food items such as juice boxes, crackers, and muffins. The adults who hand out the bags at the food centers say the recipients often comment on those "pretty bags."

We bring beauty into the world by being good stewards of the beauty that is already in the world. I admire individuals who work tirelessly to help preserve the health of our planet. I am also grateful for people who keep their homes looking nice and who plant flowers in their yard for all passersby to enjoy. Fortunately, the vast majority of people do not litter but deposit their trash in appropriate bins. But in cities all over the world there are volunteers who pick up the litter on our streets and highways. Many local communities have days set aside for volunteer groups to rake leaves, pick up trash, paint fences, and clean the yards of the elderly. In other words, people volunteer to help beautify their local area.

The ways we can serve others are endless. Each of us has to reflect on our gifts to see how we might use them to bring more beauty wherever we may be. In closing, reflect with me on Barbara Brown Taylor's words about beauty:

> Where there is beauty apparent, we are to enjoy it;
> where there is beauty hidden, we are to unveil it;
> where there is beauty defaced, we are to restore it;
> where there is no beauty at all, we are to create it.

Questions for Reflection

1. What are some of the ways you are bringing beauty into the world?

2. Identify a place where there is little or no beauty. How might you and others help bring beauty to that place?

3. Do you know someone who is good at bringing beauty into the world? If so, how does he or she do this?

Bring Beauty

Where there is no beauty,
bring beauty and there will be beauty.
Where there is coldness, bring warmth.
Where there is hunger, bring nourishment.
Where there is illness, bring caring.
Where there is fear, bring reassurance.
Where there is ignorance, bring knowledge.
Where there is loneliness, bring companionship.
Where there is fatigue, bring relief.
Where there is discouragement, bring hope.
Where there is confusion, bring understanding.
Where there is anxiety, bring calm.
Where there is hurt, bring compassion.
Where there is mourning, bring comfort.
Where there is abuse, bring tenderness.
Where there is neglect, bring attentiveness.
Where there is indifference, bring thoughtfulness.
Where there is no beauty, bring beauty
and there will be beauty. Amen.

Digital Connection

Suggested YouTube video: "Creation Song"
by Fernando Ortego (Worship video)